Fantastic Day

Morose, counter-intuitive, something of a zany, Ken Bolton cuts a moodily romantic figure within the dun Australian literary landscape, his name inevitably conjuring perhaps that best known image of him, bow-tie askew, grinning cheerfully, at the wheel of his 1955 Jaguar D-type, El Cid. It is this image that also carries in its train the stories of later suffering—the affairs, the court appearances, the bad teeth—and, speaking of teeth, the beautiful poems wrenched from the teeth of despair & written on the wrist of happiness "where happiness happens to like its poems written best" (in his inordinate phrase). Ken Bolton worked for a long time at Adelaide's Experimental Art Foundation. He edited two significant literary magazines, *Magic Sam* and *Otis Rush*. It would be an understatement to say he has published numerous books. He has published a great deal of art criticism, edited the memorial volume *Homage to John Forbes* & wrote the monograph on artist Michelle Nikou.

Fantastic Day

Ken Bolton

PUNCHER & WATTMANN

First published in 2022
Published by Puncher & Wattmann
PO Box 279
Waratah NSW 2298

info@puncherandwattmann.com

NATIONAL LIBRARY
OF AUSTRALIA

A catologue record for this book is available from the National Library of Australia

ISBN   9781922571236

Cover design by Ken Bolton
Cover art image © Ken Bolton
Printed by Lightning Source International

Many thanks to Pam Brown, Laurie Duggan, Tim Wright, Peter Bakowski
and John Levy—
who have given advice—quite clearly not always taken—and
encouragement
(that many will feel to have been contra-indicated).

Some of these poems have been published before—my thanks to the
relevant editors.
'Hullo!', 'Birds of Rome' and 'The Facts' appeared, appropriately, in the
Journal Of Poetics Research
'Travelin' Man', 'Little Elegy, 1984' and 'Wiesengrund' in *otoliths*
'Ascension' in *past simple*
'Star Eyes' appeared in *Colloquy* and was published, as was 'Letter to John
Forbes', as a limited edition from Nicholas Pounder's Polar Bear Press,
'Letter' also appearing in *Island magazine.*
'Reach & Ambition' appeared in *Cordite* and *Best Australian Poems 2017*
'Hi, Small Bug' appeared in *Australian Poetry Journal*

This has been a fantastic day

—Arnold Strals

Contents

4 Wiesengrund

1

Birds Of Rome

Birds Of Rome

for Tom & Olga

It is my duty—
or is it Poetry's (& Poetry says
Duh, what? It is *what*
I'm supposed to do now?)—my duty,
'ours',
to tell the people of the future
just what life is like
right now, in *this* part
of *this* century—& to this end
I copy passages
from Raymond Queneau (*Last Days*)
& look closely at
a poem of Charles North's, that might
complicate matters—complication being, tho,
part of the game we are shown to be playing
passing the time of our lives. Both poem
& novel argue an underlying simplicity
that is life—but I mean to show
—*here, now*, tho I realize this
is nothing of their agenda—
that the ages
still speak to each other—
1935 to 1989 to 2018.
Out the window, Via Giacinto Carini, Rome,
streetlight falls on the top leaves
of a tree, rendering them green
against the relative dark
of a building across the road (yellow,

I think, in the day) & cars whoosh
up & down, at very regular intervals.
It is Friday night. I am up,
not quite well, happy,
moved-to-write. 'Whoosh' because it has rained.
Rome has declined a little since I was last here—
with Cath in the year that rounded out the last century—
the effect of many years of bad government
& bad circumstance—tho I have nothing wise
to say about this—hasn't the West declined,
the whole Anglophone sphere?
I am tired & think a little
of Picasso. (To no real end.)
And if Rome has declined, if Italy has—&
the 'Anglosphere', & the planet perhaps—
then where does that leave me, reader of
the future?—(& reader of today—you're here
too?) *In the midst of my usual difficulties,*
that's where—

& I gargle, & go bed,
to address these issues
once more, or again, or more fully—
thru the lens—or the 'flaw' in the lens,
or whatever—tomorrow—a word,
"whatever", increasingly used
to express hopelessness, carelessness or impatience
in recent years. Often comically. Tho it is
an easy comedy. I am saying this, I suppose,
to the people of the future, before whom—these
latter—we feel a little guilty.

What will it be like for you?

Sparrows—which they say are disappearing from big cities—
are here in Rome. At least, I saw one today.
It danced & darted & sat, about the table
Cath & I shared,
around the corner from Via Carini. Smaller
& a little more russet than ours in Adelaide.
Actually, ours are more beautiful.
Good to get something stated plainly. But,
"to bed".
                    Of course I rise again
& get this started. Here. But not before
some real life has intervened—tho is this
not real, not life—it has a different feel
from wandering with Cath around Rome… A bus
a tram, some trekking & we are at Santa Sabina
& Saint Alessio's—a saint I love: held to have spent
his adult life under the stairs, a secret from his
Pa—to die on being discovered. You might. Out of
embarrassment? Regret? Tho I've led a fairly quiet life
myself, granted.
                    I rise, as S. Alessio must have done,
done his stretches, a few pressups—then down to prayer.
Not me. I strike out for the coffee shop
on the corner, a few corners away (what is Rome
if not a place of corners—open skies, curved umbrella pines
& vast edifices & blocks, of corniced & windowed masonry,
abutting at de Chiricoid angles, Euclidean & deeply
        somnolent?) order
an espresso, & sit, looking past—I calculate—the Italian Centre
for German Studies' wall—or maybe not—& watch birds
sweeping slowly around the sky.
Like a fly around the rim of a lampshade?
No. Like last flicks of a rag, around a kitchen,

a plate. The sky is empty, tho an impressively empurpled grey
    one
massed in the window in the afternoon,
behind the enormous column of the decapitated
palm next door. On which a bird sat, corvinely—
like Edward Everett Horton—
                or an ancient
Christian Democrat pollie
pleased at his situation, how far he has risen,
all those years of routine voting, producing Italy's problems.
    The palm, shorn
to a vast trunk, swells at its top slightly. There are two.
Dark columns—vertical, that swell & thin just appreciably,
appearing bodily, pagan, sensual—providing the plateau on
       which the bird sits. Corvinely.
Then hops to the roof & is out of sight.
                      What have
birds ever advised me—except *Down tools*—&
"bugger off"—
              as a sparrow once told me—told me, in almost
                      so many words,
as a tourist, in Trastevere.
                Less generous to foreigners
than Italians
           have generally been—tho in that respect things
                   are beginning to
tighten.

        (Cath notes a large street newly named for Albania—
tho most of the businesses retain their old signs of
    identification,
a more Italian name, "Aventina"—still in use by
everyone, surely, over 14.)

                                    The sparrow offers no advice
to our table—sniffs the air, takes off;
atop his enormous plinth or pedestal the crow says nothing,
hardly catches my eye, hops from it to the roof.
Disappears. And a guy, sixty if he's a day, wearing a Batman
        T-shirt,
walks down the road across the way, string shopping bag, a
        degree of swagger.
Norman Douglas, writing—on Lecce, Bari, Naples?—
in 1905, remarked the ubiquity of optometrists, chemists, &
        underwear shops—
& nothing's changed.
                        Italy is not going to solve
some of the world's problems.
                        "It's not our thing"?

Here's the thing—
                (the phrase used regularly—on an
                                interview show
I never saw but loved the idea of—Alec Baldwin
the interviewer)
                —When *was* America, by 'his' lights, last great?

What do I think—50 years ago, 55? did it peak
with 'The Morning of the Poem'?

                        "latte

                        sano"
                                        I read
                on the Italian milk carton
                & think: (feed the President some)

"gone to hell in a hand-basket", an American phrase
that, from the first,
I both understood & which I remained
puzzled by, could be applied here.

Apply here?

A Carbunkle
to your Bestertester!

       (*Mad* magazine)

Theresa May
Make Britain
Quaint Again

Da Cesaré restaurant—"ostaria" their chosen term—
established 2018—so, as it's only May now, can't be very old:
the site of a lot of smoking & standing around outside, in
high heels, tottering, puffing away, on mobile phones, sorties
      into the restaurant
& out again. We sit outside—where the presiding figure is
Rodney Dangerfield, who sits outside also, practising 'living in
      the moment'
emptying his mind, in fawn pants & bright red T-shirt. He is
      sent eventually
by the owner on an errand, to buy cigarettes, milk, serviettes,
                  maybe repark somebody's car—
& reappears after a time, sits again. Ah, Italy. Is this

love, or exasperation? The world will not be brought down
by double parking or cigarettes. "Well, it *may* solve *some*," a bird
suggests, sub-vocally, alluding to an earlier conversation. I
⠀⠀⠀⠀⠀⠀⠀⠀⠀⠀have been looking at it for quite a time—
& it flies off, message delivered.
I am hardly thinking.
A handsome kind of crow they have around here—
two-toned, black & a lighter chocolate-charcoal colour. He
watches from a distance then flies away.
Inane but highly competent music comes from da Cesaré,
some professional singing & some *Karaoke-level, 'so-so'*—(or
⠀⠀⠀⠀⠀⠀'bad')—*vocals.*
I go inside to pay & it is red-shirt, looking more like Rodney
⠀⠀⠀⠀⠀⠀Dangerfield than ever—
at the keyboard, confident, masterful, drum machine ticking
⠀⠀⠀⠀⠀⠀over

Sirens whoop & swallow the world it seems
briefly—pass—& the world is ours again, ours
& other citizens', its dimensions & routines
restored. Clamour, a vertiginous
narrowing & the ambulance is past. I write this
in the quiet, of the end of the day, on Silvi's mother's balcony,
Le Balcon de la Madame Volonta. Le Balcon
de l'Europe, a possibly fictional bar-café
in Higgins' novel of that name—one
in a long line I stand
somewhere near the end of, presuming that it
will end. *But why would it?* Beautiful, non-allegorical
clouds gather to darken with their dove-grey &
slight mauve, slight purple, a silver sky
above two principal roofs, one of orange terracotta,
the other a deep sienna. Below the orange roof—

a butter wall; beneath the other—a wall of palest cream
its windows & capitals & balconies a chalky grey,
intensely classical. Unremarkable
except that it is perfect. A bird flaps onto
a tall aerial, turns, & flaps off again, downward
like a discarded umbrella.

                    I write, I fool around, here
in Turin, on Giulia Volonta's balcony,
wondering at the point of all this embrace
of Europe's charm, Europe's ways—
it must be counterpoint to something.
("I like them: but I'm different"?)
And the sky has darkened. The
clouds have cleared—mostly—a vast
white one, miming "Boo!"

                    "Oo-*ooo*, woo woo *wooh*,"
it proclaims for its own amusement,
white in its higher parts—which must catch
the last of the light, high, high in the sky.
Here below it has darkened, various lights come on,
voices call, relaxed & inviting, there is laughter,
the purple-grey has gone,
leaving the sky its slightly smudged, thin
blue-grey; the orange gone from its roof—
now dark with a memory of warmth within.

Street lights from below lend the lower floors
a faint lemon colour. It is night—Spring,
early Summer.

                    No bird
has spoken to me—evidently—which I take to be

Torino *sang-froid*. Perhaps, after my Roman correspondence,
    they observe
my 'progress-so-far'—to formulate encouragement
or correction, as required.
                  Renato Guttuso I expect to be
coarse, blowsy, obvious—but feel I should see,
to see if there is more. I doubt I will catch his
Bar of Europe painting, so famous, or that it will be
perfect if I do see it. In fact, tho, he is better than I expect.
Also, I realise I have seen more of him than I remembered.
A forceful painter who becomes an entertainer, a
cartoonist—a reliable
fist in the air (as in his paintings)—
striking the attitudes required,

tiresomely (eventually) 'beside-the-point',

unable to matter. But, for a few decades, good.
Togliatti is celebrated. But surely his life was one long
bad gamble, chips placed on the wrong square & the choice
defended: do not form government, do not address power
                        but wait—
for the change that never came.
                    Sufficient
to count as tragic?—you become a near-hero, a loved figure,
for embodying the national dilemma. ("I coulda been a
contender," said the contender.) "Of course, the
alternative... ?" ask the birds wisely.
"Poverty, dissension, violence?"

A death-mask profile of Togliatti in one continuous single line
seems loving, respectful & forgiving—a head, as if lying,
    pillowed.

How introduce these things—Queneau's novel, North's poem—
or re-introduce them: did I say I might? In Queneau's
early novel the intense young man, a student, near the end
is reconciled to the world: he attends for some twenty minutes,
in a small square—where a man smokes & reads,
stretches, smokes & reads again, where housewives
shout to each other, a cat appears & moves from here
to here, a dog barks, a woman's voice is heard to sing;
the cat, the dog again, a bell. The student
considers all this as a philosophical problem—whose terms are
dissolved or defeated with a repetition of these events.
North's poem 'A Note On Labor Day'
consists similarly—of scenes & sounds, sounds
particularly—& things seen, or imagined, as their
explanations, their source (the horn of a truck, a
car backfires); pigeons a number of times
are dispersed, fly & regroup, a bike is stolen,
fish are imagined to have crossed the bay with the night,
taxis come & go, while North expounds a philosophy,
or a view of things—that places him at their centre
at peace, unconfounded.

                              Queneau would have known
he was
'on to a good thing'—

to help conclude his novel—which he folds away
after that point, the student's 'problem' resolved.
Charles North was pleased with his task
as a challenge, I would guess—& he brought it off. It shares
a family resemblance to the poems by his friend, Tony Towle,
but is less drawn to the Augustan discursive's 'machinery'—
        more

W C Williams & Edward Hopper. It is dedicated
to his wife, a painter. Paula.
                              What is the relation
of these works—
to *this*? None that is close: they were supplies I took on,
in preparation for the journey, lucky charms.

Turin will not seem to have furthered my case,
but it has altered my mood, moved me a good way past
my introduction. A highly cultured city. The first,
almost, in which I have experienced the interior of a
          representative
Italian apartment: its large & calmly ombrous rooms,
sparse but fine furniture, parquetry floors, absolute
intelligence of design & disposal of functions & objects, its
discretion & sense, its calm. Torino is an orderly city, likewise
… of long arcades & treed corsos—like the lovely Corso Vinaglio.

Laid out on a grid, on flat ground, it takes days to orient oneself.

"Trees wave on the roof
across the street
which has the forsythia for two weeks
every year, which I always want you
to paint, which is past,
or almost, as light sweeps it"   etc
                              More
Schuyler than Williams—(or Tony—or Hopper).
"Which I always want you to paint" attaches to
the forsythia I think—& it is 'the year' which is

past. I like it for not bothering to be too clear

"So a tugboat has plowed
up Broadway pulling half
the Battery behind it" — which I am not
New Yorker enough to be sure of
—or to see how it is possible—
but like a lot

(What is the relation of the novel, the poem, to this?)

Torino.
We may never have entered the Bar Personal but meant to.
Those we did enter we liked—where we rested spending the
        traveller's
quiet moments, gazing at the trees outside, watching the traffic,
watching others pass.

                        One estimates, judges, measures
one's surroundings, insulated from the problems of the world,
failing to catch the eye of the beggars—who are relatively few.
We have little money ourselves. Giulia & Silvi could be said to
        live
well, but frugally—out of habit & philosophy. Silvi will pay
to study, having relied on scholarships heretofore, will waitress
as she goes—& become a useful professional in areas
of foreign aid, immigration, population flow—
a remove from her Australian years as a greenie.
Our own children plan second babies—& careers
that might be safe but cannot be sure—the worry that attends
modern life. We visited a town in England that celebrated
its having lost half its mass

to the sea in the 17th century, blind
to the fact of imminent sea rise that will surely see the rest off.

We are in Via Pessina, four floors up—fifty paces, seventy?
from the student bar & restaurant area—& which changes its
      name,
'Pessina', for Via Toledo, the street Stendhal proclaimed
most exciting (the happiest?) in the world—or was he so
      realistic
as to limit himself to "Europe"?—& which in some respects
must not be much changed—as well as much changed. New
      drinks, new trinkets.
Sri-Lankans appear now in numbers, a significant presence—on
      Sundays—clearly
their day off, from what one guesses will be menial work. It has
      bustle still
tho the excitement might now have moved to the streets &
      alleys around
Via Constantinople, Porta Alba (&) Gesu Nuova. These,
      anyway,
are raffishly glamorous. Naples.

There are no trees—& hence, especially given the traffic, no
      birds—
except at Tom & Olga's,
who look down on a private garden, whose luxuriant green
feeds many. Otherwise we see—pigeons, if we walk thru
      town—
a lone hawk circling high, cruising on rising thermals,
above the parklands of Capodimonte. The hawk has no advice
      for me.

The city beneath consists of monuments to its own
        oppressors—centuries
of aristocrats, foreign despots, bankers, two thousand years
of the Church: palaces, baroque cathedrals—
backdrop to the theatre of energetic Neapolitans.

                                        What, I think, can
Sicily teach me?

                        For long moments, at night, I
content myself with the view from the balcony of endless
        streaming traffic:
pearls of light—the cars, the motorbikes & vespas—as they
stream & weave endlessly & variously down the hill below us,
phosphorescent against the dark night,
taking my breath away.

Sicilian Addenda

The triumphant fashion victim presiding over
The Good Shoe. They were good shoes & he made them.
The shop oozed Eurotrash good taste. Quiet & dark.
Men's shoes in half a dozen styles a quarter of them
in colours. The genius of the place a very spry
seventy year old with well-cut
straight wispy silver hair, shoulder length. An
amused smile. A black-blue linen jacket over expensive,
white, collarless shirt—& black linen pants, tapered fairly
        tight—
ending a good four or five inches
above the ankle—sockless, in handsome black loafers
with a tiny bit of tan trim. One liked him.

He was in on the joke. The other staff were a tall & muscly
young man, & fairly busy, & a beautiful darkhaired
young woman seated in a deep deep chair, not
about to move. She too liked his humour.
Where are they made? asks Tom. China. China? But the
designs are Italian? Chinese. Chinese, but why? My
father was Chinese—ha ha ha. Girl's eyes light up. She arches
the foot of her crossed leg. His look is great: the fabulously
got up serving of a look that quotes 'Picaro', Tom Sawyer,
urchin, carefree bumpkin & says "Many euros"
Yachts! Lamborghinis! Yes, I do know personally
Jeff Koons. And Mimmo Paladino. Madonna. I have shaken the
        hand
of Robert Gray.

#

The old 'tourist' part of Taormina (home once to Nelson,
        Goethe,
Nietzsche, authors, intellectuals, academics, actors & actresses)
is nice to wander thru—but only early in the morning.
Unfortunately, nothing is open till after 10.
From that point it begins to fill with the young
& the old—mostly well-dressed in resort wear, unlike
us—not so many of the *thirtyish*—unless they open boutiques
set out restaurant chairs (trattorias, ristorantes, enotecas).
The press of people in aimless procession tests one's—
        everyone's—
fellow feeling. A few are conspicuously glamorous, tanned
bejewelled & coiffed & accoutred, including the odd girl
cresting her 'top model' appearance, often part of a
wedding party.

A quick walk behind our house & up the hill is the much
more pleasant reverse. A wide apron of concrete
overlooks the valley, precipitously, like the rest of the town.
On it a large number of kids & parents, run, ride
& jump & throw balls, the adults down at heel
chatting & happy. I watch for quite a while, from
some steps at one corner—like the oldies outside the
        supermarket
at the other, that I passed as I came thru. I am reminded,
searching for comparisons, of Larry Clark's photographs,
Pasolini's Rome. So I like them, of course—the single guy, the
old couple under the awning at the store, the mums talking to
each other in the small parking area across from it, & all the
figures crossing paths, running standing walking, joking &
        calling.
A few kids approach me at different times, pursuing a lost
ball, or out of curiosity; one tiny, many-curled blond boy
        needing
respite from the crowd (is it 'madding' him?). *Buona sera*,
I say to him & smile. He looks to be three or four—& asks
me something & I say *Me dispiacere—non parlo Italiano*,
which he must have heard before. He looks at me differently,
        smiles
again, turns, goes down the stairs & joins the big picture once
        more:
groups & skeins of figures forming & reforming. Pleasingly
        random,
ongoing but not repetitive. You'd come here every night
(7 to 9 o'clock) & sit in the cool, watch them. I've seen the same
        people
sitting outside the store before. Here for that purpose.

An afternoon with friend Maurizio.

He takes us to an old town, once moderately large—some of it

—including a huge church—built in 1200. Mostly run down,

with narrow

streets & covered walkways, lots of it falling apart,

overgrown—but

the Taormina money—richer Italians, others—are buying in:

one passes old nonnas sitting on doorsteps, consumptive

looking men,

cobbles & bricks misplaced & a general bleak grime, to come

upon

large, startlingly well-lit chemists, beauticians,

bag & shoe stores, jewellery shops, nightclubs: intermittent,

or in clusters. A ghost town soaking up new blood,

being revived & taken over. Two Italys—one decrepit, the other

bearing Audis, BMWs, Porsches, expensive scarves &

sunglasses, good shoes.

Randazzo—the town. Why should Randazzo stay impoverished—

to remain picturesque? What will happen to Randazzo's poor?

(Or is the change largely generational?

A disappearing act.)

#

Two large seagulls on the roof opposite Maria & Mike's,

they stretch & dip their necks—a spooning motion—

& make a long sound followed by a few small

rattling sounds, that is very like the beginnings of

a kookaburra's call. Appropriate, because I'll be

heading back to Adelaide in three or four hours.

The drive last night around town in Maria's Bambino—1974—
engine like an old pencil sharpener—a sound of small pebbles—
has Rome appear miraculous & charming again, magical.

"Taking"—to quote North—
"my breath away"

Note

To have formed, after the war, a Communist, or Communist-led government,
as Togliatti might have done, would have been to forego the Marshall Plan
money that reinvigorated Western Europe. On the other hand, Togliatti
also allowed the reinstatement of rightist, Fascist judges to the judiciary.
Government was handed—for the next forty years—to the Christian
Democrats as Togliatti waited for the culture to shift, as he believed it must,
necessarily, leftwards and his party be handed undeniable legitimacy.
Australia's uninspiring post-war politics responded to similar pressures.

The Facts

& in tribute to the following and their works—
Tony Towle, the books *North* and *Autobiography*, and the poem 'Works
on Paper'; Charles North,and his poem 'A Note on Labor Day' from the
book *The Year of the Olive Oil*; Raymond Queneau, the novel *Last Days*.

I buy only one thing—a five euro hat,

against the heat we expect
over the next few weeks,

& because I see one that doesn't look too awful

The one I choose—(black)—has the effect
of looking vaguely sacerdotal, without
convincing anybody that I am a priest.
In it I feel a little like Paul Hewson

whose efforts to appear hip
I always applauded,
tho no one else seemed to
Of course
I never knew if Paul liked me,
or noticed—or cared about—
my applause. It wasn't, in fact, that I thought he
was hip
so much as I thought his unease modern—
& his will-to-hipness somehow admirable
(or hip in itself), a sort of
ascetic, priestly & austere vocation.

Do I, in my hat,
'recall him'?

 In London I more or less decide
to write the poem. Tho before we left home
I had figured *to write something*—& had taken
Wayne South along
as a possible spur or model.
 In the poem I *do* decide to write
I decide also
not to resist too much the cliche of
'the-poem-in-Italy'
 Tho, without wishing to succumb to it
too much, you inevitably do. You give it play
'for decorative purposes'—

ironize it to maintain 'distance'

Or it's the enemy
& you stay 'well away'—

But wanting to write something
was the overriding factor. Ambivalence
'got a look in' was as far as realism went.
We arrived sick in Rome
but in a good mood,
from London where we froze.

Rome was warmer—a week into May.
But Rome presents in so many ways,
that fail to cohere: the down at heel
the wealthy, the inane, the cool

the foolish monument to Victor Emmanuel

the romantic ruins—of the baths, the
Aventine—the fabulous river—Testaccio
& Trastevere—(the latter now wasting
in parts to a shadow of itself)—so incoherent,
or disparate, *that it is hard to meet foursquare.*

It was nearly twenty years earlier we had known it.

I liked it even so—& in truth I had
only ever liked it in parts. I liked them *then*
& liked them now mostly—
& found some new—& then we
were gone.

Turin was nice, very—
but less a world city, less a city
one 'had to come to terms with'.
It was admirable—I was smitten by it
& our time there was terrific. Then Naples.

I read Henri L'Oupöl in London.
Ultimos Dias—& in Turin I wrote the poem.

I had started it in Rome. But in Turin
I had nothing to read, so I wrote—

& bought Zadie Smith (*Swing Time*)
as I got on the train to Naples

—a book I increasingly withdrew my investment in—

a re-write of her own *NW*
& Elena Ferrante.
Unconvincing. In Naples I saw
Guido Reni's terrific 'Atalanta & Hippomenes'
& a late Caravaggio that reconciled me to him—

the Roman works seem 'all over in a flash'—

a blinding clarity—& then there's 'nothing to look at'.
This had mystery, a softness to outlines, details

that swam to you from the darkness, that waited—
for you to find them, over time, by accident.
Christ getting a scourging, I think. You could
look at it forever, or repeatedly. Other things

were there, some Carracci, some Bronzino—& Artemisia,
& Jerome taking a thorn from a lion's paw.
There are some great churches—
but I hate them for what they are. Also,

the art history I was taught, its
whole framework, was Florence, Rome,
a little Bologna, some Arezzo etc.
Venice.
But not the South. Hugh Honor,
Duveen, Berenson

all too well brought up, & bred
too delicate—for the South & Naples

None of these buildings were canonical—
tho some must have rivalled Rome
in splendour & conception.
About the paintings one knew only

Ribera, & the Caravaggists almost as a rumour—
a dark, 'intense' Catholicism was cited, & the explanation:
Spain, the Inquisition, a simple, stark 'faith'
& a consequent darkness.

                                        I read, in Naples,
Updike's *Rich In Russia*. It is funny. How great to find it.
I haven't read him since *Rabbit, Run*
in 1969, 68, or 70—& had thought
he 'only wrote about rich people'—or money—& in a sense
he is: his novelist-hero is 'paid in roubles'—

but this was funny & not entirely unlike
Gilbert Sorrentino, even, in some ways. My
hero, sigh.
Sorrentino is black & scathing & irresistibly selfconscious.
Updike is smooth, & light—but clever. I will search
more of these out—the 'Bech' novels.

[I buy the hat in Naples, take it to Sicily.]

South's poem is hardly a model available to me—
but I turn to it as something to read
in the pauses in my poem—& occasionally get an idea—
from it, or at least *while reading it*.
I hadn't thought much of South. But I pulled out his book,
A Year with Popeye, one I've had
a decade or two, & hadn't liked—

&, giving it 'one last chance' ("Come on,
South—
save me from boredom"), find this terrific poem.

More research & I find others. South, South—
I never knew ye! I'd preferred his friend
Terry Tunes' poems—& now I've found South, or
'true' South.

# # #

[[[SOME POSTCARDS

BEN SANDO

Dear Ben,
I guess you are, as I write, saving the animals & their little lives—
but maybe doing it for somebody else now, as an employee & not a
—what? sole trader? (which sounds like someone sailing up a river,
laden with furs—chug chug chug—& here you make jokes about 'up
the creek' & 'sold down the river'.) Your Vet's business sold? This
has been a good trip tho the highlights I suppose conform to the
outline of cliches, despite actually being highlights. 1) I saw a guy
berated for eating his food off a Richard Serra slab—best, he didn't
argue that it 'wasn't Art'. He lifted his plate & made the *What you
gonna do* shrug & said, But there was no room elsewhere! 2) Saw a
Renato Guttuso show (good artist becoming a bad one over twenty
or thirty years) & 3) a great Guido Reni & a great late Caravaggio.
Otherwise, Cath & I have eaten & drunk & laughed. And *we* should
do the same—some time in the second week of June maybe?

Ken

JULIE LAWTON

Dear Julie,
I love you, & I have always loved you—ha ha ha ha ha. And it's
true tho, isn't it, in a way? At any rate I have always wanted your
approval. Italy is great—tho you would not approve of me in it,
it is such a joke. London tho *was* great—& you'd have liked it a
lot—so many people fiercely themselves & confident. Richard &
Suzy send their love. Their new home is very nice, it backs on to
Hampstead Heath—& they seem in good shape. We're with Tom
& Olga Sankey in Sicily. Mt Etna just outside the window, Olga on
the phone to her son. Anyway, it's cheered me up a whole lot. It's
time we caught up. We'll issue an invitation when we come home.

Cheers, Ken

NOAH BANENS

Dear Noah,
I wonder if this card will get to you before we do? We think
about you lots & figure you would like it over here. Italy is
beautiful & dirty & nuts—& *you're* beautiful—terrifically
handsome anyway—& usually need a bath—& you're definitely
nuts. You should come here one day & bring the whole family. Is
Arlo coming along well, are your Mum & Dad? Say hi to them
from us. See you soon!

Ken & Cath

MICHAEL & WENDY

Dear Michael & Wendy
I wonder if this card will get to you before we do? Am thinking
about you lots [ETC]. Italy is ... [Repeat Richard Serra thing]
ETC

Ken

MICHAEL & DI

Dear Michael & Di,
I wonder if this card will get to you before we do? We think about
you lots [ETC]. Italy is … etc [Repeat Richard Serra story, Guttuso]
ETC

                                        Ken

                            #   #   #

In South I like the dependent after-thoughts or
early impulses, first guesses—
as to where the sentence is going—allowed to
attach themselves, to hang
from the sentence's main thrust, weakening it
comically, they give a kind of indirection,
a dagginess, a rivulet becomes
a slender trickle &, its last gasp, the sand absorbs it.
But it has moved in interesting directions in its course.

As South employs it, tho, this is a virtue: Labor Day,
a day in which he sits, passively, & New York's sights & sounds
            & 'incidents'
encircle him, a sybaritic St Anthony, happily 'tortured'—by
            felicities.
I emailed South something to this effect—
                                        about
his sentences' indirection—but heard nothing back. He
probably figured me for some smart-arsed critic, a type his
poetry goes out of its way to inveigh against. I concluded,
                                        Say hi
to Terry Tunes—we used to be in touch, to suggest I had once

38

been in the loop, but it may not have been enough.

Do they not

still talk? (The great Tunes poems will never be touched.

Galling for a poet sort of similar. (Of course, if

he's galled, what am I? (In respect of *either*—or both?))

Weirdly Tunes' first 'real' book was called *South*—published

well before Tunes & Wayne met, I think. *True South* might be

a title, for a book on South's virtues & vices (more the vices)

& the kind of harping criticism Tunes might like to make. I

could write it. I might mention this to South. (Ha ha.) Hmm,

wouldn't want to get dished by those guys.

In London I think—or did I even start it on the plane out?—

I began with a statement of the poem's intent, its contract

with itself, to describe the real conditions

of life in this part of the century, while traveling

in Rome, Turin, Naples—& acknowledging

the probable, the possible, or destined influence of South—

& his poem, 'A Note On Labor Day'—& with the *proximity* at

  least

of L'Oupöl's *Ultimos Dias*, both of which, I hinted, hymned the

  quotidian,

or hymned its acceptance.

I looked out the window (palm tree), listened (ambulance)

& began. At this point I was in Rome.

A bird,

my sole piece of 'machinery', could tell me what to think

whenever I needed a pause, came to one, or needed to return

to the fanciful—or needed it undercut… by a bluntly spoken

bird—an avian Groucho, or Oscar Levant … a name it has
    taken me
some time to dredge from the past, a past watching television,
the bedrock of my education.

We were living, in a slightly unliveable flat, in a very good
location, that gave us some *new ways in* to areas we'd known
    before,
& some new locations, & allowed some of the *old* ways, too.
Rome was more unkempt this time round—some of
the old thrills were absent. I still liked it.

Realism was hardly one of my goals, with Terry Tunes
somehow at the back of this—invoked as the shadow *behind*
    Wayne South—
& perhaps *still* the stronger influence. Would I have read South
if not for Tunes? Tunes' neo-classical periphrasis & ornament
do hold the real—but as if in huge & ironising pincers.

My own work strains for that tone, or something of it,
but does it ever hold anything in its sights, its grip, for long?

Can it ever keep a straight face—except in those moments
    overtaken
by an unwanted solemnity?—An 'unwasted celebrity'?—There
    is

no place for him at The Good Shoe. Tho I am 'reminded'—well,
I was—of a faint stain on my grey T-shirt that I have washed
    twice

but not yet removed. It grows fainter—& by the time I get
home
may have disappeared, weeks—an ocean & a continent—too
late. (Do
you 'know' The Good Shoe?) A kind of status-quo regained, to
paraphrase
Milton, whose shirts were *very likely* much stained. Talk about
'anxiety of influence'—we were, weren't we, talking of it?—
Milton worried,
a lot, about whether he'd have any. "Look, John," I'd say, "even
now, your name…"
etcetera,

putting my tiny shoulder to the wheel … for the good of all of
us—
Milton,
me, Robert Grey, South, Tunes, even L'Oupöl

Turin was fun, thanks to our hosts,
Silvi & Giuli her mum, tho we were not quite well—
& Naples was great, & great to catch up with Olga & Tom. In
Sicily

we could breathe again—& there occurred 'the lifting
of my mood'.

\#

The successive birds I began to find rather repetitive.
Not objectionably. Uninventive.
But invention, what is that, isn't it one of those
rhetorical categories? Aristotle, Horace, Leon
Battista Alberti? How old fashioned.

Here in Taormina there is the bay—as there was in Naples.
(Famous, tho I made no mention of it.) A handsome, white
cruise ship has just entered. Six-thirty a.m. Gleaming.
Soon the town will be filled, with couples favouring beige.
In fact, a tiny boat has just departed & heads portwards
perhaps to seek permission from some authority, the
        harbourmaster,
there might be something half-ceremonial about it, it being
        Italy.
But at 6.30?

"Name of ship?" *The Isola Bella.* "How many?"
Two hundred—and fifty. Usually fifty stay on board. "Okay.
I'll alert the police & the pickpockets."

South used to have things cross the harbour—
a squid or a mollusc—an oyster? There's a tug
he suggests has drawn half the Bronx with it, a
momentary illusion or fancy he doesn't deny. Better
is a rodent—a raccoon?—that drags a woman, somehow, after
        it.
Along with things genuinely seen, or see-able. These
make up his poem.

Do I even have a dog in mine? How unimaginative.
But imagination, what is that, right?

#

I start this, with various people standing behind me—
Wayne South, I suppose, for one—
& Kenneth Koch behind him, which is bad news for South—
Koch will have almost certainly donned

an ape mask, wave an outsize toy elephant gun,
poetic parrots mounted on his arm, his poetic head. Anyway,
with them there—defining
a middle ground, *becoming*
background as I move forward, the
subject of my poem—
I might now have your full attention,
or as much as is reasonable to expect
just a dozen or so lines
in
to a poem of boundless, tho admittedly groundlessly held,
ambition—*not held firmly either*: a sort of feckless
'feeling lucky' feeling. Me, not you—tho you're entitled to feel
        that way too,
if you feel it.
Your feelings are sort of to-the-point,
yet *not* the point somehow—in the same way
that a stake is necessary to the game but it is *not* the game.
I mean (Do I, do I mean this? Well, I do now—
but I didn't), 'bale out' in 'media res' & 'leave me'
—lost, in the middle of a long afternoon, at a
dark wood desk, or bench or 'table' ... outside this
coffee shop, The Middle Store—Wayne South (black T-shirt,
        dark glasses),
Kenneth, in a loud, & wide-checked, sports jacket of
pale brown & yellow, Terry Tunes, sitting sullenly beside them
(thinking "This must be miles from Tribeca—what are we doing
        here?
They're driving on the wrong side of the road!")

                                        Alan Wearne,
                                            more
                                        vastly amused,

sits apart from them at a nearby table.

                                      So there you are.
(In the sense of 'get the picture?') I am contemplating
a *Krazy Kat* cartoon—just a single frame—
                      that I have here
as a bookmark—while trying to recall another
from memory—a fuller scene: more sky, more rock-face, cactus,
empty space, tumbleweed, dark shadow.
Coconino County, Arizona—& work out
how I feel about it. Cartoons 'hang' upon,
isolate & exaggerate, one single point,

which they nail, thru something that is not quite 'resemblance'
but is something like it. (Recognition is our response
to it.) 'It's a theory.'—Well, a remark.

But the great cartoons—often, always, characteristically?—
nail more—& Krazy is an example.
Krazy's is a 'world', with lots in it, that we recognise—
& love. Something else—Charles Schulz's *Peanuts* for example
('much loved', sure, sure), has less.
                        Naturalistic drawing
can be held to be 'finally' an abstraction—a notion I can
hardly entertain, just barely can—but works, we feel,
by what it packs in, a plenitude of recognisability,

but with a cartoon element disguised within it, by which it
nails something … that gives the picture its character, its
charm. Here Manet's portrait of Berthe Morisot
meets Herriman's Krazy—both liquid-eyed, trusting,
                    worried
(in black, typically). A brick bouncing off Berthe's head?

Hardly. I love that painting. Wearne,
Terry, South & K.K. are all looking down the street

where a car—driver lost in a deep fug,
brain fizzing—has circled, dangerously fast,
the traffic roundabout, allowing me

to slip away, mount my bike, ride home—& pack for Europe
                    where Cath & I 'go',

'fly', in a day or so: London (Richard & Suzy,
Wendy Griffith), Rome (Rome, beloved Rome), Turin
where we see Silvi—& meet Tom & Olga in Napoli.

The four poets, all chatting now, rouse themselves & walk,
Alan in the lead, to The Little Fig, I think—another coffee shop,

Terry expounding on his 'Works On Paper' & its relation
to 'Epistle to a Patron'. Something like that. He looks chuffed,
draws himself to his considerable height—gestures generous,
          eloquent,
expansive—grandiloquent almost.
No, not that—but grandiloquence is within sight, all three
contemplate it, with satisfaction, the idea being less
          troublesome
than the, um, the item.

London.

Then Rome.

Birds of Rome

("It is my duty—
   or is it Poetry's (& Poetry says
                              ... ")

2

Hullo

"Hullo! (Yours Cordially)"

"Yours cordially"
—Ron Padgett

I address Ron Padgett,
& sign off—
"yours cordially"
tho "in fact"
(to quote Ron again)
"I am a wild palooka—
in a half-lit office,
hair crazed etcetera,
wind-up mice playing in the hall"

And Tony Towle—
whom I envisage, as
I always do, at a window—
a window &
small balcony—
looking onto a view...
inkily black, white
curtains either side,
that move slightly in the breeze.
          I stand beside
& behind, my hand
on his shoulder.

          The unconscionable thing
about this stance—my *mental* hand,
not my real one—anywhere, any time—

is the implication the
person behind 'sees' the same thing—
philosophically—as the more forward figure
(why the latter,
                    so often,
shrugs the unwelcome hand aside,
turns indoors). Anyway this image
never gets beyond the single gesture.

(I don't want a fight with
Tone.
So I don't 'go' there.)

(In my mind.)

                    (Which is the only place
                     I go anywhere!)

Who else do I address?
Am I really going to
'address the poets'? The
'Great dead'? Those 'alive'?
(but major in my mind—
"in *my* mind, at least")—
them?

                    And why?
It is not as tho I haven't
done this before

                    And while it is true I am
                    happy to repeat myself,

is it one of my strengths—should I
'play to it'?

                    Nope.

And I have nothing much to say
beyond hullo & 'carry on' &
I Like Your Work.
                    Plainly—tho I hope
it is not too plain—it claims a kind of
parity.
          "Bonjour M'sieur Courbet"
probably did the same,
                    for the artist who painted it
—Gus himself.
                    Tho he had
the courage
of his illusion
                    & pictured his landlord
greeting *him.*
                    Do I imagine Towle, Ron,
anything but puzzled
                    were I to make an appearance?

That's as may be.

So whom?

Not
the NY Schoolers—'the young'—
tho the young are older than I am,
are now aged.
And not the first generation either.
Not Ashbery or O'Hara or

Koch. Jimmy Schuyler
I could almost address—we
feel we know him, his writing
so personal. Altho we don't

(but everybody reads him, right?)

He wrote on,
into our time,

he kept his themes,
ostensibly,

small—tho they weren't.

                              The four
felt themselves
part of American Poetry—
a small field right then: Pound,
Williams, a Beat or two.
Not Olson really, not San Francisco.
Maybe John Wieners. I am summarising
I suppose, O'Hara's views

                         They thought
they were it &,
as such, addressed themselves
to the World,
maybe *not* with the expectation of a reply

The second generation, like us,
come into a larger field, of
many poets, a smaller stage—

a smaller share of the stage:

they would be 'New York' poets.
They published after O'Hara died,
the 60s & 70s & after. So,
our time.
As America's true poets
O'Hara's friends addressed
world literature—Europe's
(... barely England's, but Continental Europe)

      —where the young crowd,
by contrast, cleared their throats
& spoke up (Ron, Anne, Ted,
Tony, Bernadette, Kenward)—
for local recognition, if that were possible—
& not with confidence—tho with cheek
& grace & humour
              watched television
listened to pop music.
                  Like we do.

Address Peter Schjeldahl,
the irascible? Not likely.
            Joe?
But Joe's gone, & Ted.

      These people
are major to me—not the host
of Pulitzer Prize winners, dud
laureates, who 'stride the stage' over there.

Not the Faber Oxford Cambridge
candidates —

     "Faber published it
     so it must be good!"

         or the Irish

             I am stating
allegiance here, or placing
a bet—on the future: that the
truth will out.

I like the way each nation's
literary establishment
rules the roost at home
but internationally are written off
& the real writers come into their own.
Billy Collins, Sharon Olds? Not for me.

Craig Raine? No way. Tom Raworth, Maurice Scully!

             Eileen.
     #

        Tradition
& the Individual Talent. Tradition
& the minuscule talent.

        (Tradition & mine)

        Will

my work be counted? Not really.

#

Violins.

["Powerful nations have great poets; small nations
have tragic poets. *They do our dying for us,* whisper
the powerful nations. *In this way we produce great poets,*
whisper the small."]

But this is a little 'rich' — & sort of mittel-europeany.

#

Are there
points to be earned,
standing proxy for
'Australian Verse'—

enacting an anxiety
that may be my own
& not 'the nation's'?

Are there, huh?

But "points to earn"?
What to do with them, how
cash them in?

In any case, I am not standing-in…

I hardly seem to be doing any
of this addressing, either.

Would I address Australian poets?
(aside from Cath, Pam, Laurie)
Probably not. And not the elders,

who—too obviously—relate
to no past, have no future:
the provincialism problem

                              failing as we would fail,
                              an imitation of life

                              I am going to make that mistake, too
                              better not watch too closely

Australian literary history …
will be 'one thing after another'
(Henry Ford's phrase—
or was it De Mille's? Anyway,
"they had *our* number") : a succession
of styles or epochs focused on
action elsewhere, approval that would
never come.

                    ("Epochs"?!)

                              (The Epoch of Rodney)

                              (imagine)

(The Rodney epoch,
the Les.)

If I'm not standing-in,
perhaps I represent no-one,
quite naturally?
I went as a teenager once
to a party & was too afraid to go in.

I stood outside.

A suburban house in a North Shore
suburb,
lights in the windows, loud music,
talk & laughter coming out.

I am still that guy?

I suppose I do address Pam, Cath, Laurie
tho in the direct & literal sense. I send them
a letter—well, an email—
send them regularly. But—
as I mean it here—
I do *this* less regularly. (And do I address
the literary figure—'Pam', or 'Cath', or 'Laurie'—
or the person I know?
Mostly the latter, I think.
Do I attempt to gauge the difference?

Should I not ignore the first, address the second?

HOW OFTEN DO I ADDRESS *ANYONE?*

but

ACH! HAVE YOU *SEEN*

THE COST OF STAMPS?!   Ha ha.

Yes, "ha ha" — tho anachronistic.

Who,

these days, uses stamps?

\#

(On a TV show a night ago
a woman character said
"the loneliness of men—
you can feel it coming off them")

[[use public library: the Scottish/Italian quote re human faces]]

\#

(the Scottish/Italian quote
I could look it up. I could find it,
you would think)

\#

So I'm not standing proxy.

\#

"How's it going?"   —is that the question?—

asked supportively?

Am I, as charged,

(That is, somebody said it)

fascinated

by the distance between

us ... &

America, the world? & do I 'advert' thereby

—(that is, *do* I?)—

to the sensed oddness of our endeavour,

Poetry?

(—For how, for whom, for why?)

(Mental?) Australia

pretends not to care—but it does, watching

'casually', as it waters the lawn, polishes the car,

brings the washing in, asking occasionally

how it's going. Again I remember the guard

on the bus in *Lucky Jim*: "Well run, whacker!"

as the hero—puffed—leapt aboard.

Am I fascinated—as that someone said—

by 'the distance between',

... more than with America per se?

Maybe so. What do I know of America,

aside from details that attach

to special interests—popular music, some

old movies, details of the lives

of the poets I've liked, learned

thru repetition: I have no interest in the Southamptons

tho I know about it/them—know
very little, but *some* things—& so on—
(isn't it where the rich go, to piss on, look
at their big abstract paintings, chill?)—
vague ideas about various locales, Bolinas,
Bleecker Street? Where else? Gem Spa? Not really.

Where have they gone, the loafing heroes of
folk song? asks Kundera

I am like those Japanese soldiers,
continuing vigilant, long after the war is over.

Or the distant member
of a far flung, minority religion.

Hanging, in my hammock, lazily.

Maybe I am too lazy tho
to be thinking about America?

Apparently not

There's a distance between us & it,
as between us & the horizon—
with which it's co-incident: a
vagueness, luminously humming.
Not the place, but the rumoured place
just beyond, of the great

#

I like to recall *those who went before*,

I shun *those who came after.*

Their heroic pursuit of tenure.
I guess no more reprehensible

than the bookish — as they
used to do — taking Orders,
or becoming a courtier—or,

for that matter,

grubbing for reviews,
commissions, from the BBC etcetera ...

opening a small mobile-phone
repair shop—or selling books like I do.

Their books, even.
Hullo there, Language School.

#
More & more I am decided—today, at least—I don't like Michael
                                                              Hofmann
—his criticism nearly always wrong.
                              #
            "every word pronounced in the world goes on
            being heard forever. Has mankind always lived
            in such a resonating shell?"

                                        And I address

these poets again

                  address 'the idea' of addressing them—

for who could actually bother
                    ... 'to do this thing' ?

I address them:

                              tho it is months ago
a month a go
                    I began this address
                                        What did I
intend to say?
                    Kick on, Ron   —   How goes it, Tone?   —
that sort of thing.

                                        The neighbour,
the 'peer' in today's language
                              — (here indicating
                                                  not
a member of the House of Lords,
                              but someone like me,
another punter) —
                    nods,
                              before he bends, turns
the tap off,
              drops the hose,
                              to indicate *Well done,*
carry on
                    (If this were England, here
I would get off the bike—the figurative bike—remove
my cycle clips, aware maybe of pigeons
wheeling overhead, the small garden plots
attended nearby, a factory whistle—

(the last maybe still in the area)—

but this is Australia.
                    (And as it happens I do
get off my bike
                    —an anachronism?   a weirdo?
another punter?
                              chuffed tho.

                              #

                    chuffed but
                         #
                    but chuffed
                         #
            chuffed a little, chuffed a bit

                              #

& offer this poem

The Hamptons

Consider your Rothkos!

                              #

                                        We don't use
"whacker" much,   never did
                              tho it would *seem*
Australian enough, would fit our mouths :
Why not?

            ("Wanker", I guess, absorbed it.)

Whatever I was called, I accept it—
In fact, it was just a nod—
Nothing actually said

                              reasonable
                              approbation

(from the bus driver, a Sikh I think—
would he have called me whacker?)

                    #

Was it America so much—
so much as History,
and our distance from
that?

          #

Pam flies in today

(I will talk to 'X' in person!
Maybe write him a letter,
or her—(let's be
fair for a sec)—talking, & writing,
at the same time—
addressing them ('AN OPEN LETTER
TO X') a new,
funny kind of Personism,
lacking in authenticity

address it, check the address,

add stamps etc.   Hang the cost!)

(They need never know!)

(But I digress.)

#

(Ah, the mice.
Out of the hall?
or wind them up again?)

#

The 'elders' of my own time
fade into a kind of canonicity

Like abandoned billboards

The canonicity doesn't look very stable—
Or very satisfying, if it comes to that

But I don't care—
or I try not to.

Les

Adders
            Tranter
Gray
            Maiden

Young Michael, a kind of

wistful, winsome
Bob Newhart figure:
satirical

#

Douglas Stewart was alright (!) —
who talks of him?

#

A billboard outside a country town,
advertising *The Silkworms*, blows in the wind

shudders, rocks back and forth
faded, peeling,

bullet holes in it,
brown bottles & broken glass scattered around,

long grass, a burnt out car.
Further out

similar buckled tin leans back from the sun:
bleached lettering and imagery announce coming attractions

attractions that have come
& are long gone

A Weatherboard Cathedral, 'Golden' Builders,
The Alphabet Murders, A Cool Change, other
harbingers … of salvation, of rest, belief

And there's the guy playing me!
I look a little bit like Ben Johnson
in *The Last Picture Show*

standing for something
but I can't tell what.

It's a bit part only.

                                  (Bryan Brown in the main role
                                  walks on his hands along a bar.
                                  There's a drink balanced on his shoe.)

Personism

Pam,

                    The best way to read the *LRB*
is at one sitting!
                    usually between 11 & 2 AM.

& if it's a good one
                    I always have the reflex urge
                                        to email you
saying so.

                    —(too silly?
            But there you are)—

                              When I have this thought
I then remember
                    that we might, without
realising it

            —conceivably—

            —(well, not *very* conceivably)—

            one day sing in unison

                              "I'm going to German' /
I'll be back some old day…
                    etcetera".
                              (Who else

                                        sings this song

but you & me?)

Anyway, HOW ARE YOU?   (To get
                        my underlying purpose
                                        —disguised
as a formality—
            out of the way.)

                        Pam, dear.

And wasn't it a good issue?
                    The review
                        of the book
                                critiquing
CRITIQUE'S
            'HERMENEUTICS OF SUSPICION'.
                                (I think Eagleton
                                        thank god,
didn't once mention Christ.)
                            The piece on JAMESON'S
CHANDLER,
            the account of the German Left's
                            shift to nationalism
(only some of which
                I fully understood), much of the Brexit
hand-wringing,

                Even Alan Bennett's
                            Diary piece (I tire of him,

sometimes,
        but not this time).
                    Marina Warner was almost
readable
        —tho I had to jump ahead, skip bits—
she gives herself too much space. Or 'they' give her too much space.
(Is she their 'space-filler', replacing Jenny Diski?)
                              She used to be
good.

(By the way, I attach a probably
              —scratch that, read "possibly"—
'final version'
        of the Triestine poem
              'for you'.

                  I think it is improved
          enough

     & shouldn't change a lot more.
             Shouldn't *need* to, tho it might—

             might change)

                (First time
I've ever used the expression
           "Scratch that.")
(I think maybe
      I WON'T USE IT AGAIN, either.)

        (It felt weird.)
          #
           ("—from

The Purity Of Diction In English Verse.")

                                                            #

                                                (A book I
love the idea of you reading.

                            I see you throwing it
across the room.)

                    ('A' room,

                                        some-where.)

                                        I think I am
going to have to *think a lot harder*

                            when writing—
or think a lot more *between* poems—

                                    than I used to.

                                    Depressing thought.

                                            Used to be
I could walk up the street, from the Eaf,

                                    or sit at my desk
late at night,

                    & just start in.

                                That's
                        what I'm thinking.

                                                    I won't
mind.

            —IF IT WORKS

                        (If it

                        would 'begin' to work)—but I'm

hoping it might.

Thank you

for supplying the images

for Andy's

'LET'S GET LOST' project.

For some reason

it was a mildly

depressing experience, writing that stuff. I suppose because I

DIDN'T WANT TO DO IT.

I'm nostalgic probably way too often—

but not about that particular

stuff, our early days.

(Not as a matter of policy.

I even like it

when you or Laurie do it)

Given that I

didn't much want to say it,

I hope that piece is not too often quoted back

to me.

(Ah, literary history.)

(And then there's

one's own life. Unreal.)

Triestine

Hi Pam,

Here is the poem for you.

Begins poem

What to tell —
what I've been doing,
thinking about,
reading,

B) things I've noticed
... that crop up,

(to be dismissed,
& RETURN,

Halley's comet fashion,
to my 'consciousness'
so called)—

things
that dealing with
would make seem 'major',

that seem full of meaning
I can't grasp

(tho I can *focus* on them,
slow them down

& they revolve slowly before me

staring back

buried, & banging on the wall of their cell

hoping to be heard

'We're in here! Let us out!'

Prisoners

of some mental Zenda,

The Man Who Laughed?)

A message

from my psyche to my waking brain, to attend maybe.

Screen memories.

I take a step away from them,

adroitly

like

a star from Mineola Prep

—the dance academy bit, of Mineola

(as opposed to, say, 'track')

'adroit', right?—

Things empty, but emblematic, these

bits of consciousness.

The Spiritual in Art ?

#

Ah,

The Blues Brothers,

("Do you see the light?")

the Marx Brothers

as they

ham it up down on the farm,

Paul Robeson (?)

\#

That is,

I never use the word / without inverted commas.

\#

I read Tabucchi

—the *Porto Pim* and *Fra*

Angelico volumes—

& Jan Morris on Trieste & 'Europe'

do I keep a distance from Europe? No way, I
LOVE the place —ha ha— but I do, of course.

Trieste

she says

is pompous, creative, raffish, melancholy
& 'out of the race'

She loves it.

I've been twice. I love it. Opulent,

faded

ruled out of relevance,

(as she said,)

& melancholic & beautiful.   I saw the city name on

suitcases as a kid.

                  (Or so I think)

                       & imagined it remarkable

                                     —before

I'd have known

                 what

              to IMAGINE

                    to imagine that—

                                       a

port city. Then "ZURICH PARIS TRIESTE".

                               Modernism.

                                   Dada,

the old world & shipping lines …

                        her earlier book on Trieste, its subtitle

the Meaning of Nowhere

              Those tiny, empty apercus

                          they occur maybe

most of them

          looking out a window

                    Maybe Trieste

is the best place for them

               They are 'grounding'

But I flee being tethered

                floating,

free, & nodular

           or nutty

Watching clouds roll by

       Writing to you

      (I guess if they were apercus

      they would 'reveal' something)

Letter To John Forbes

"My dream a drink
with John Forbes
we discuss the code of the west"

Excuse, John, the liberty I take
   in addressing you like this—you'll
pay the price of authority, make
   the allowances an author must.
   I'm a fan. Still. And was, too,
your friend as well, in later years—where once
you'd seen, in 1976, a rival—though one

you'd have thought not quite your speed. Who else writes?
   I'd like to know. Alan, Gig, Laurie?
Pam thinks of you often enough. There are young types—
   young middle-aged—devoted to your work—& the young truly
   for whom you're a hero, something your large frame was duly
suited for. Does Morgan write? Mark O'Connor? Not
the bathysphere poet—the poet of depth & altitude, who got

a dithyramb written or perhaps a haiku
   while on a bungee jump, a terse sonnet sky-diving—
the real one, of wit & intelligence, who
   helped you write 'Admonitions'. Him.
   The other guy shaped once as 'Mr Poetry', appearing
everywhere, writing under sea or upside down—
forgetting the most important thing would be what he wrote.

Then he promised a poem for the Olympics
    & all went quiet. And I think I haven't heard of him since. Has
he written, to push, maybe, spelling reform, enlist
    support for it? Ha, ha. I imagine you answering him, as
    if in pity, "Mate, ..."—a plainspeaking but relaxed
mechanic—pointing out, as you would in the 70s, that a poem
must be 'crash hot'—anything less was under-done. 'The poem'—

or as in Berrigan—'The Poems'—how that phrase
    as we would utter it expressed a sense of formal
& ontological reverence—a feeling for it as
    a thing apart & something higher. You'll
    not find that much anymore—the poem as text or
discourse reigns. As poems got longer?
as workshops 'tolerated' the thousand puny blooms, poems

crabbed, unresolved, spavined, inert—poems that
    faded long before they ended tho one remembered vaguely
their one good idea? (Tolerated 'for the sake of argument'—
    or to avoid one?) I heard that, unbeknownst to you,
    you'd 'never get a job teaching'—for being too severe, too
likely to favor the very few. I also hear
Melbourne or Monash were about to offer tenure—

good pay, position & superannuation. A
    new life would beckon, changing things forever.
You might have taken it, & the pledge, & kicked on?
    Being dead is very superannuated, & we'll never know
    how things would have gone—John Forbes in smart clothes?
No, but secure, professorial. It takes no imagination to see
the advantages of how things did turn out: an early exit,

not too much tapering off. John, I will say,
   I've been looking at the late uncollected poems
& *they seem very good*, & characteristic of you, your way,
     from line to line—but, un-characteristically, unconcerned
     to clinch an argument thru closure & balance, concerned
rather to make the argument, or arguments. 'Uncollected'—
so maybe not. They seem hardly to be bettered

as a 'kind' of thing—if you could bear abandon
     that first ideal—of 'nailed it', of triumph & perfection. For what,
intense, sustained intellection, politics? On
     what grounds did you resist—if this is what you resisted—'crash hot'
     tops 'exciting-&-compelling'? The absolute
tops the merely actual, the theoretic, the workaday useful?
Taste, nostalgia maybe—for an ideal, that I think though

was no longer serving you, or was proving unavailable. Sorry,
     that was meant to be a question. Though the whole point,
the constant joke, underlying Auden's 'Letter to Lord Byron', surely,
     was that Byron couldn't answer. If I rolled & smoked a joint
     right now, would that help communication—or anointed
my throat with 'neck oil' (Laurie's one time term for beers—
mine for retsina) would that help? I think you'd like my mind clear.

Much as you liked a drink yourself, & probably a smoke,
     that was your *mind*: you'd not want mine any vaguer.
I toyed, John, initially—with addressing Byron, or Auden (or both),
     but couldn't choose between them—or imagine the way the
     conversation could go, even possibly. Samuel Johnson? He tho
reminded me of you—tho a more comic figure.
I won't talk to you *as a joke* (I never did). We were in this together—

Poetry. In this poem I should 'tell you things'—
  to be funny, to cast an angle on the difference (slight?
or telling?) between now & then, soliciting,
    by implication, your answer. (Does Tranter write?
    I remember once your addressing him with some hostility
as 'Jack' which John affected not to notice. A tense moment therefore.)
For me: I'm in my 'studio'—a room built on since you were here—

'safe', except from the perils of age. 'Safe'
  is how you saw my situation—not incorrectly, not really
unkindly, tho you'd got my number: *Adelaide, a safe
    haven.* It still is. Cath & I got back from Italy
    a few months ago & while away I wrote on 'il bel paese'—
Italy as the literary experience her—meaning
to parody the genre, & mentality—& not demean

the country or the Italians—as you'd appreciate: *they're not us
  but they're terrific.* Of course I'd query that "but". (But "and"?)
Maybe "consequently"—or does that overstate it? 'Birds of
    Rome' I've called it—& added to it a fine example of 'coat-trailing',
    a phrase I associate with you. Your relish for it—its meaning,
its antique provenance, & for the *practice*, I think. That is, tacked
to 'Birds of Rome' is a (mild, mild) provocation (tho it amuses me), 'The Facts'—

which tells of the writing of the 'Birds' poem,
  the procedures, shifts, pre-assembled devices;
their poverty, & my assessment of them; the poem's
    hidden agendas—of mild rivalry with my exemplars,
    of ambivalence: would they care? they must care?
would they notice?—& in a more dispassionate key
the tourist's experience: *Italy & how we got around it.*

Larkin, in 1960, opined that "in some way, Auden,
    never a pompous poet, has now become an
unserious one." You were always a serious poet, the poem
    aesthetically serious (in its challenge, its target) and,
    where 'formally relaxed'—your Auden mode—better than
Auden, but totally serious about the content—
which was what? *Australia vis a vis Europe:* our edge—

their edge—'Europe, A Guide'; *existential*
    pleasure, & risk, sensation, the body—'Drugs'; &, in 'Anzac Day',
Australia, class—our history of decline & erosion, the Labor movement. All
    these last have continued, in ways that would have disappointed but not
    surprised you—as they have disappointed but not surprised us. A nut
now runs the U.S. *What's new?* you'd say. But this guy is something else.
(At the last minute you could 'see it coming'.) But your surprise

would be like ours. It's not so long. Twenty years.
    The devolution one 'regrets'—or is appalled by—but it
has been ongoing: the major parties so resemble each other there's
    no mechanism to change direction—we exit,
    individually, the actual & withdraw to merely commentate, tweet
salving critique on social media. Quips (so many words
I associate with you, John: "our quips so cool, so various")—words—

our sole response, everyone joining the commentariat
    none remaining as the polity. Rome burns.
Shaun Micallef, First Dog On The Moon speak things clearly,
    awful Alan Jones—shock-jock—finds & turns
    a scuffle into a race riot, instructs a PM "Repeat after me," forms
part of the creep-&-fogey alliance that fires that same PM,
selects another stooge. Penny Wong should lead Labor—but then

that would be to side with intelligence & to gamble
   on the intelligence of the electorate: but Labor under Beazley
(& ever since) have not wished to explain principle
   nor stand by it—allow the populace to regret queasy
   choices & vote, next time, for a party that had stood for something.
Instead a new face fronts crossed fingers & depends
on the metronome—the swing back, their way. Reith sends

a phone call to Howard a week out from the election
   reporting 'Babies overboard!' & Beazley's victory is thwarted
More of Howard—whose argument against Keating had been his intellect—
   who here wins by saying, *Look! over there—what bastards!*
   & just enough Australians *who-would-never-drown-a-baby* voted
for it. Howard could laugh. It never happened! Polling showed the populace
firming behind Rudd against the miners but then he was gone, a new bunny was

chosen & was *effective*—&, in her turn, would have won—or lost honorably—
   but was ousted: and voters saw the Party would stand for nothing.
The right-thinking right were in again. Julia Gillard gone. You feel, probably,
   hearing this, you left just in time, or—if you're used to it—that a return, if banging
   on like I do is what you'd be reduced to, *is not to be considered.* Actually, writing
in these 'strict'—not that I'm strict about them—'forms'
might be the surprise. Not my forte. The difficulty spawns

'variety', I suppose, & indirection: the comedy of getting
   nowhere quickly—irritating if you don't get a laugh.
Am I providing them, or ideas sharp enough to keep you listening—
   'reading', if this is a letter. At least my idiom is closer to yours: parts
   of Auden's letter to Byron would have left the latter hard
pressed to understand him: the idiom & the matter.
Then Auden told all about himself. Would Byron care?

I wonder what you'd like to know? What girls are wearing now,
  how the various Rugby League teams are faring, your contemporaries,
how they go? Women look great, always, & mean to,
    but they're tired of that expectation—as I think they indicated, maybe
    some time in the 60s? (Rugby League—it's rarely shown here,
I don't follow it. It's become a dumber game—even as the players
have gotten, objectively, better. Of your contemporaries a few are stayers—

those I've named. A few have stopped & who can blame them.
  I kick on—but plainly I've got time to kill. Keating,
your old favourite? Keating remains the dark prince. I remember him
    lecturing the opposition on the history of their thinking,
      their traditions—their heads lowered, in shame, embarrassment (they didn't
know)—ending with a funny school-boy 'rude' noise, a joke about them
skiing downhill, eyes closed, no poles. He remains private—

yet the only of them to reveal himself, share with us
    unguarded—as equals, smart enough to get it. Of Turnbull
he remarked, you'd need a microscope to find his 'ethical values'.
    Byronic, wronged, he doesn't say much, has still the dark, slightly chill,
    glamour, lives we imagine in a castle, or like Batman, tho neoclassical,
fine-suited. The Fat Man—Sydney Greenstreet, Fats Domino? Oh,
Murray. He seems now diminished, has run thru

his various guises, all claiming the principled victimhood of some minority:
    'country bloke', real Australian, virtuoso plain-speaker,
marginalised redneck or yokel—neglected Anglo-Celt formerly—
    for a position on some spectrum. Which may be so, at last. The poems
    often resemble a sort of baby language—to reveal his wonder,
innocence, capacity for revelation, epiphanies, apercus.
The own-goals, & constant bungling, of the West in the Great Game—this you

would have attended to, & our complicity. Our foreign ministers
    you'd have cherished—Downer & his air of stammer, of blithering,
Julie Bishop's show-pony, best-girl competence
    (the earrings & tailored clothes), Bob Carr—how he *rose*
    to the occasion—& Rudd, after years of talking down to us,
was about to, patiently, talk down to the United Nations. *Look at me, Ma!*
They must have objected, or seen it coming.

In real life we never talked this much—a half a dozen letters,
    some visits, in the 90s, to Adelaide, to Melbourne. We discussed poems,
yours & mine—specific ones—their successes, their problems—
    that they solved, half solved, worked with, were damaged by—
    or survived, or skirted. Gossip. Not much else.
So I owe you this letter.
If you were still here—or here again—you'd hop a bus

beachwards. Sydney beaches—they're still magic
    & the people, the young, you'd love. I do.
It's been noted, I think, how atmospheres,
    the feel of air & weather—on the skin, or thru
    a T-shirt—are in your poems: sand, concrete, tar; blue sea, blue
metal, macadam; bats & moths & bugs & traffic,
perspiration, the lungs—part of the gift to us

from you—that we liked, as we read the poems,
even as we saw it as incidental. But it remains.

3
Others

A Saturday

I email Brian & Jennifer thanks

—Ella & Tim arrive soon
in town from Melbourne—

'finish' more or less
The Saturday Paper

a paper waiting out the lull
in domestic & political news

addressed to readers
also waiting it out—

The early days of Turnbull.

I will need to find
something else to read

The purchase a token — of 'belonging'

(to the chattering class)

(a *would*-be member)
(the '*would-be* chattering')

I look at the Japanese poems
Leith's translations, the one about

the boxing gym, the
'loneliness of men'

—or their 'signing on'—
to fight, & punch, climb

that long lonely mountain
a sorrowful destiny

Days before, I lie doing stretches
when—near, & above, her

back to me—a tall blonde girl
punches the mittened palms of her trainer

& enquires about boxing,
how she could get into the ring—

& her trainer *and* the boss
(hitherto uninvolved

but in the room),

are very keen to advise her
(join a boxing gym, train hard—

& be patient—a good gym
will look after you,

you won't get a fight for
quite some time, & so on)

She leaves & they
discuss her & their advice. A

'male' province, they have been
unable not to

claim it, possess it

(Young himself, the boss
recalls for the other

the first of *his* few fights,
the adrenaline & fear, the

uncontrollable excitement)

The Japanese poem (called 'Men')

"The Kaneko Gym on the Odakyu Railway Line is
A small
Boxing gym
At night
From inside the train
I can see people training in the Kaneko Gym
Young men boxing
Within the black night
Blossom-pink muscles
Like cherry blossoms sweating silently
Boxing, in their movements
A stray memory comes to mind
A memory I seem to have had

Can't say for certain
'KANEKO GYM, NEW BOXERS WELCOME'
This is
Always
Read silently
By those with heavy sodden hearts
They
All
Open the dark door
And
One after
Another
Have gathered
There"

(Masayo Koike)

It is a great image—the distant,
lit gym   —   the 'men'

Viewed from a train
wondered about

#

'Integrated Health'
                                   —across the way
from where I am
                        (the Korean coffee shop)—

has a stone Buddha in the window who rests his
leaning head   on the palm of one hand

'wistful'—like the carved wooden figures tourists
bring back from Bali. Related?

("I've never seen / a Buddha like that,"
                                              I think.)

I check the 'Format' gallery-&-coffee shop

                                        a *would-be*
'going thing'?
                          But maybe they're 'THERE' (!)
                                achieving lift-off,

the crowd looks sufficient
                                    Still, I pass on,
for the familiarity
                        of my regular spot

(for this *would be* a poem)

                                        plan
my LIFE OF JOHN HOWARD

                              It will involve
no original research

& a tone something like
a snide Nazi book-burning

did they run to snide?

Gilbert Sorrentino — (*Gold Fools*) — my model
scathing incredulity   is what I'm after

#

Coffee & salad

& I make it back to work
to meet with a real poet

neatly turned phrases
similes that ennoble

Lyric-&-Pith

(tho more pith would do).
An interview.

Then I think again
(about the boxers)
& Masayo Koike

the kind pity she feels for them,
an empathy that counters the will to satire

Similarly
I might watch

a tiny John Howard

—at the practice nets

facing up to the bowling—
bruised, blocking and swinging, confounded—

glasses steamed-up askew—

as I rode past in a train.
Empathy I doubt that I have

Poem (*Ascension*)

a stick moves across the ground, leaves circle & rise
the great ominous sounds of *Ascension* as it begins

& I am merely 'up again', at night, reading — bits
of this & that, looking some things 'up', making

a list. "I spend my days in picture galleries solely,
& that's why I'm so melancholy." I am not

melancholy. The theme for *The Honeymooners* & for
The Jackie Gleason Show come next & I have an image

of Jack Rose standing importantly & conducting
those few bars on television black & white his suit maybe

a little large for him aspirational this was the nation viewing
I wonder did Frank O'Hara care for Gleason maybe unlikely I

did. As a teenager I knew it was a world passed already,
knowable history saying goodbye Jackie's face wobbling slightly

as it went under, slipped slowly away, full of knowledge
that was then not now. It is a long while since I have watched

a *movie*—black & white—with their earnest propositions

what was "the pony of war"? who to ask? Will
we ever know? I see Crab tomorrow night, but I won't ask

I am really an Indian at heart—beneath
"a hazardous settlement" & these the wings of an

extraordinary liberty which I know & know
only now, not forever—as I rise. Not tough

like Frank. With none of the warmth of John Coltrane.
But alive.

#

a stick moves across the ground, leaves circle & rise
the great ominous sounds of *Ascension* as it begins

possibility invests the stacked, piled, fallen
books and CD covers on the desk, the quiet, blank

computer screen. I pick a slender *mittel european* novel
read rats run in the roof — or maybe possums

(not much cleaner worse when they die) —

birds I can hear still, the extending summer night.
I rise

free, move thru the darkened house —
with me, Coltrane, O'Hara, Pam Brown

#

a stick moves across the ground, leaves circle & rise

cloud builds, roiling — stills, like
a move in chess   the implications, now, contemplated

The light branches, of the hedge, outside my window
scrape fitful across the glass—stop, start.

A sound like worry an importuning
the great ominous sounds of *Ascension* as it begins

But you are 'other'   move thru the house
The fridge's hum's concluding

Of 'no moment' — but yours, & actual — the skin's
slight moisture cooling in the night air

Beyond, vine leaves, street light filtered thru jacaranda

#

a stick moves across the ground, leaves circle & rise

& I am merely 'up again', at night, reading—
the music's themes   repeat themselves return—

like characters in *Solaris*, worrying, plaintive
their suffering ennobling — read this, answer that.

The Rauschenberg I look at—'Pilgrim'—
beside the fridge magnet

(Given by John—bought in Prague,
gravity the O'Hara must counter)

Days ago I wondered
would O'Hara have liked the music I was playing

& figured no. 'Sidewinder', 'Speedball'—too heartless.
'Star Eyes', on the other hand, would be okay. With him.

With me. (Am I—really—an Indian?
O'Hara at least could ride a horse

sit one.) A letter on my desk from John
requiring an answer. To its left the dark &

focused stare of the handsome young man who is Kafka
(John's memento)   near a small,

too-blue reproduction, of Rauschenberg—'Pilgrim', 1960—
& books, by O'Hara, Maurice Scully, Lee Harwood, Saskia Beukel

Tony Towle, Adorno, Chris Nealon, Tabucchi, Pam's new one,
Cath's & mine—& tapes, mostly 'live', of Speedboat.

the motifs repeat—the great ominous sounds
—of plaint, or suffering?—a kind of hand-wringing—

like the movement in the wind, of the hedge outside,
saying What is to be done? What is to be done?

a stick moves across the ground, leaves circle & rise
the great ominous sounds

as I read.

On First Considering Chapman's Homer

Famous, right? The ball I remember was pitched fast
but not at absolutely fierce speed
& dipped a little pulling across the batter's
right side. Chapman was bent at the knees
& crouched low himself, straightening
as he swung. He hit it hard, almost
too close to the end of the bat. The ball
surprised him I think, floating wide. He would have
meant probably to drag it across a little &
to have hit it lower. I saw his eyes watch
perplexed for a moment then he ran confident
the ball was going all the way. It was
out of the ground, the cheering of the crowd waxed a
second time at the realisation that the ball was 'gone'.
Chapman was gone himself soon. He retired,
opened a bar down in Texas, little place called
Darien. He called it *Chapman's Homer*—
popular with literary types.

Reach & Ambition
Five Poems Derived From John's Photographs

for John Jenkins

Reach & Ambition

Late at night, up, looking at
the things on my mantelpiece
a profusion of crap, clutter & gewgaws
a range of detail I love (John's photos of it
came today, reminding me). I look at the pictures
blu-tacked there, above—postcards of paintings
1900 to 1920s mostly
but some Manet, some Fragonard, a Boucher
Michael Fitzjames, a Chardin—a piece of paper,
yellowed, proclaiming "*Honeymooners* star
Meadows dies" (with a picture of Art
Carney, Gleason, & Meadows), a picture
of James Brown being 'assisted'
to his feet
by a Famous Flame, a large photocopy picture
of Pam, 32 or 3 … Anyway, the Manet—
two white camellias glowing
against a black ground—makes me think
Look at things! & on that basis
I think I will search out
the book of Manet's flower-pieces
& then, depending what that does to my brain,
re-read the Tranter poem I find,

placed in the back of this book. 'Loxodrome'.
And maybe I will

II   Gone

        Left of the mantelpiece,
beneath the Chardin (a small, be-suited,
silver-haired boy—regarding a spinning top
on the table before him), four
tiny spots,
of blu-tack,
form a rectangle
where a stamp should be—a patch of torn envelope
& the postal stamp that was on it. Gone. John's photos,
tho, reveal it to have featured a dalek.
U.K. recognition for *Dr Who*. I am relieved.
For months now I have been aware
of the missing stamp, & had looked about for it,
thinking it showed a Chance Vought
Corsair, a fighter aeroplane of WWII
that I had liked. ('Liked'.) I had been a fan of the plane
in my teens—& surprised to receive its image
as an adult forty years later stuck on an envelope,
& looking so American, mid-century & 'of its era'.
I don't know who had sent it to me
tho there are only a few candidates.
But now I see it is only a dalek—was only a dalek—
& I care *nothing* for *Dr Who*. The fighter plane
will show up one day, within a book of poems,
marking a spot to return to—in O'Hara or
Towle or Berrigan, Padgett or Mathews—
& I will be surprised & admire it for a second

III   (Further)

                Further right—
beyond a photo, from the outside,
of the front of the house at Westbury Street,
where I lived nine years—a photo
Mary gave me, the house white, window-sill
& door pale blue, maybe the fancy iron lacework
at the eave below the guttering blue too
the whole framed by the green leaves of a tree,
the wood of the tree an angled dark accent
at the right … Anyway, near it
are some designs of mine, screenprinted
or water-coloured, & some pictures, with figures
(it occurs to me now)
grouped in threes.
One, rather Pop, shows a mother & father
clean-cut, at a restaurant, flanking their son—
the cartoon 'Bert' from *The Muppets* who looks
straight at us, while Mom & Dad look right,
alert to … a nightclub act? a waiter?—
something outside the picture. Of course
Bert looks bizarre. Above, women clean up the Reichstag
after WWII—three women, it appears—in fact
three pairs of women—bend, mopping or shovelling
at rubble, dark figures, shapeless,
dwarfed by the immensely tall
pale Greek columns of the ruined building.
Beside Bert & his parents, a photo from late 19th Century:
"The Match-girls' strike: their pay was docked
to erect a statue of Mr Gladstone" says the caption.
High-waisted skirts & tight, formal blouses,
all with hats—their best clothes—one looks pretty

& all look aggrieved & sure of their cause—
then a Braque or Picasso abstract—smudged,
glowing grey, & brown, & white, of a kind called (once?)
hermetic

IV 'Loxodrome'

John's poem, John Tranter's poem, 'Loxodrome', I was
about to call it 'Lucasade', is great.
On first reading I was conscious
mostly of its easily maintained urbanity
& its complexity, charting a move
from North to Southern hemisphere—
in a corkscrew motion?—via visits to certain
'places'—New York, Paris, Australia—
& poetic *spaces*—Baudelaire, Ashbery-&-O'Hara,
Forbes—& to poetry readings & events, & then
his response. It includes two pieces of
information I recall giving John, knowing they
were his kind of thing—about Freud
& Arthur Hugh Clough. Now I read the poem
closely for the sense & grammar
of the construction. Good to have that clear.
In the poem John imagines me
spying on him thru the fence—as
he cleans the pool, pointing out
annoyingly, a leaf he has missed?
Then John Forbes, in JT's dream,
notes an error in one of his poems.
In fact, I see a change that could be usefully made
myself, tho not necessary & I doubt
I'd point it out. "(R)ecalls, for us, a tireless

mechanical rocking horse / galloping evenly
over the heather, the rhythm / soothing
& slightly narcotic." Would that be better?
Maybe not much. Maybe not at all.

V   The things JJ liked

The things that John must've liked—
(tho he liked it all, the confusion)—
at one end of the mantelpiece a small yellow
monoplane, high-winged, its propeller & wheels
of a like yellow—an infant's toy—one wheel
a little broken. It sits, like everything, wedged in,
between jars & dishes (of paper clips, pencils), pencil sharpeners (one
—one of these—in the shape of a nose), small bottles I must have liked
—for their shape & colour—two 'metal' milkshake holders
cast actually in ceramic, one with a bunch of pigs-bristle
paint-brushes rising out of it, like flowers from a vase.
The second one (both are mauve) has a small flyer
for a piano recital on Cortula or Hvar.
Ivan Pernicki—tho Ivan Pernikety
I preferred at the time. (It got rained out,
cancelled. We were going to go—the posters were all
over the island: Chopin's mazurkas, I'd like to think.)
                                                                In
what looks like a small urn—ceramic tho it pretends to be
                                        woven brush—
(coppery orange)—is a perfectly round
white or flesh-coloured ping-pong ball, with
a face painted on it comically menacing & ghoulish
with a black top hat: its amused eyes rest
just above the urn's rim. (It's mounted on

a toothpick, I know, so you could stick it in things
(food? A cake?) & was given to us by Yuri's
then German girlfriend, Kathleen, from Dresden.
We never met: we were overseas: but she liked us—
liked Yuri—& left some presents for the house.
There's a clothes brush I never use. Some stickytapes,
small staplers, a book cover—grey, proof copy—
for Pam's *Fifty-Fifty*. There it is again, nearby,
in 'full' colour, & a vase from my childhood—
& perhaps from Dad's, or did he gain it
as a wedding present?—
a toffee-brown, with a scene painted on it—
people sitting in an 18ᵗʰ century farm kitchen:
tables, chairs, an open fire
a bonneted woman sitting in a niche
against the wall knitting: passing time, but busy.
Back at the other end, near the plane, some
rusched paper snakes—that I think Sally Forth
gave me: they're broken now but still look serpentine—
in fact, even more so. They were attached to sticks,
& almost invisible thread allowed them to move,
snakily. There's a Paul Sloan painting—an image
on a postcard, behind the snakes (just below
Bert *et famille*); there are two Singer sewing machine
'light-oil' containers, why? & a picture by Micky
(Micky Allan), framed, of
a curiously carefree footballer (a goalie, I always think)
failing to make a save. (There are goal posts, pennants,
an indication of a crowd, behind.) (Late in the day—
or maybe it's early in the game, but it is
how he intends to go on.) Right near by,
on the door of the clothes cupboard is a colour photo
(from the *Guardian*) of a guy—on the wing—running

full tilt, the ball (Rugby) clutched high
against his chest, skinny—head thrown back
ecstatic that—by his lights—he's going to make it,
just, in the very corner in a moment. It says,
"David Humphreys scores one of Ulster's two tries"
He looks like he's missing some teeth. You want him
to succeed. The crowd are yelling & laughing.
He could easily be bundled out, you would think,
but he's going to make it. I love it: human frailty
simple pleasures. What else?—Beckmann
(*Lido*). Martha Reeves & the Vandellas (beautiful
in very funny pants) Richard Widmark—
in a sixties suit & hat, narrow tie, pressed flat
against a wall, expectant, gun out—two
Joe Louis postage stamps, Stendhal, pictures by
Kurt, & one by Sal, a photo of The Nips—formerly
The Nipple Erectors—posed in the street, the lead singer
in a zoot suit, slightly crouched, legs apart, the sole
girl in the band amused at the boys' antics
stands very still, holds her guitar, smiles; a drawing I did,
of a hat, for *August 6th.*

I did it

here in this room, under the fluoro, at the desk.

There's Rauschenberg's

chair—

combined with the painting, & Seb & Mill
& Mill's baby, Hec.

Another Morning—Species Of Spaces & Curious Items

Cretin! I think —
>> of the man in the abnormally
decorated hat,
>>> waving as he progresses up the street

to imagined admirers

>>>> Uncharitably, I guess.

Are Australians naturally stupid?
>>>> New Zealanders
say YES
>>> Maybe the two countries
know only the others' dumber exports, or
the unloveable
>>>> — sportsmen, expatriate
>>>>> failures

like the guy they let build
>>>> in Christchurch
>>>>> & other places
with fake credentials
>>>> Shirtdinger?

was that his name?
>>>> But some great people
are walking by this morning,
>>>> a thin woman taking

very small steps
                    a little as if she were sliding
                              them forward
her head hardly lifting
                         weird retirées, a

small tour group of Asian students
                              being inducted
somewhere
                    attractive young women
                                             young men
with curious curls &
                    beards, beards, beards.

I'm reading Perec
                    Species Of Spaces

Two girls who have adopted a very slow pace
(but quite long strides), carry coffees
abstracted as one talks
              looking off to her upper left, thinking,

the other—*also* sightlessly—gazes at the ground
& listens

an impression of eyelashes & small noses
                              beautiful cheeks
shoulders squared
                    the long cardigan on one drops
to calf-length
                    both in pale jeans

Laurie's poem today

one, he says,
I found.
I remember writing to him about it
saying I was mystified, I think, that I had
(apparently) not liked it
when it was first sent
—how long ago?—
Now I loved it,
I wrote.
And, re-presented with it, he liked it too

I rise,
bow to the crowd

Shaun Kirby, Deep Farceur

"A racehorse, isn't it?" — *Adam Cullen*

"A writer of the serious, or 'intellectual', farce?"
— *Susan Norrie*

"Arise, Sir Mice!"
— *Ben Jonson, One-Eyed Jacks*

Since the mid eighties Shaun Kirby's work has changed a lot—
    though it coheres mightily and its coherence

Has much the 'appearance' of a densely fortress-like structure,

A castellated, buttressed siege building, a forest of tall and
    closely packed firs, or the 'castle' perhaps of a
    Coney Island.

Unlike much difficult art—though exactly like much of the
    best -

Neither fun nor profundity is absent from Kirby's pieces.
    Some are funny 'even'—sure—some are affectingly
    tragic or stare *at* tragedy as if 'with' us. (Insisting,
    "Look!") The

Key to Kirby's works—and this is not a key so much as a
    formulation of mine that expresses only the kind of my
    bafflement before them—

Is that they have the feel of screen memories about to be
    cracked (a sudden insight, we feel, will explain them to us)
    or at least see them

Revealed *as* such. "Screen memory" is a Freudian term for a
    recurrent memory the subconscious throws up, to hide,
    substitute or *go decoy for* memories that must not reach
    consciousness.

Because, Kirby's rebus-like pieces (sometimes bristling with
    clues, in a seemingly text-like charade—or at other times
    un-

Yieldingly minimal—opaque, confrontingly dead-pan,
    denying, yet grinningly confident of, our return)

Describe or emulate *the morphology* of thought and
    understanding: its fumbling, convulsive manner, at one
    moment stymied at the next naming an

Equation that had not been apparent or that loomed like an
    accident about to happen, an uncle one shouldn't mention
    yet who

Even as we lowered our eyes cleared his throat—*and then*
    "It's Uncle

Pete!" A gasp from the conscious mind when we wake up but
    here, asleep, Pete seems completely, now, one of the
    family.

Firmly Pete nods and tells the story that it is as if he has been
    telling, and re-telling, for ages: he is in a carriage, the
    scenery rocketing comfortably by, jawing to a stranger
    when the stranger's eyes light up at something innocuous
    Pete has said, with *"a wild surmise"*. This is clearly a
    'literary' phrase and events seem to pause—the wide eyes
    of the auditor looking on—while Pete considers it—only
    to be woken by the conductor pulling at his sleeve: *wild
    mice, sir* the porter is telling him, have been swarming
    across the tracks so that the train has slowed and will be
    arriving late.

At once the screen memory, the image of Pete's sister, our
    Aunty Esther, saying "Perestroika", or discussing the
    Petrov scandal, or something similar (which

Reliably ended the dream at all times before—*our* dream, not
    Pete's), presses its

Cheek against the window of our train of thought, head
    turned from us who are the assembled clues who long had
    gathered to break this case—

Esther, we thought, was one of us. But she had held steadily
    to the key. Bereft of it she stares

Unhelpfully at the landscape that rushes by in the dark
    outside. How can art be like this?

'R'—the letter that begins this line, unhelpfully—like Esther—
    is no help. Merely interrupts. *How can art be like this, in the*
    gallery's bright light? That is its talent. In the master's
    hands.

Richard Grayson
The Life & Times

Being the life & times
of one
Richard Grayson,
artist
&
wit

I would have that drink now!
— Arthur Rimbaud

Early Days

Richard Grayson was born and grew up
in Hull where, as a baby, his godfather
Philip Larkin, the Laureate of Hull, on
frequent visits and after many a jar
dropped the wee bairn from his knee, producing—
as mother Grayson had predicted—her young son's early
and seemingly *permanent* resistance to establishment ways,
and favouring of the avant-garde, in contradistinction to
the elderly Larkin.

the elderly Larkin.

School consisted
of attempts by Richard to put his tongue
down the mouths of certain girls
(who proved uncertain of the benefits of same),
and the acquisition of a formidable education
and the wearing of it lightly, the habit of study, the knack
of using cigarette and lighter, with nonchalance—

and other social graces (becoming use of corkscrew
and of bottle opener, for instance).

Further Reading & Premonitions Of Fame

The young Grayson attended
art school, and there investigated aesthetics, drugs
and the more legal ways
of deregling the senses—much in the manner
of the Laureate of Hull—and dreamt of fame. *Note*
an early, tangential pass at fame: an acquaintance
of RG's was once in the same room as part of Lou Reed,

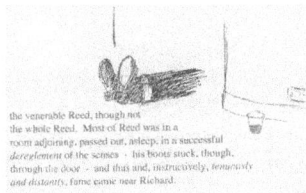

the venerable Reed, though not
the whole Reed. Most of Reed was in a
room adjoining, passed out, asleep, in a successful

dereglement of the senses—his boots stuck, though,
through the door—and thus and, instructively, *tenuously*
and distantly, fame came near Richard.

*F*ame beckoned yet again in the form of David Bowie—
who would record as a flip-side a tune part penned
by Dick Grayson. Money would roll in, limos
would deliver Dick to parties—where drugs would be
free, women too, probably—& David Bailey or some other
     tosser
(right?) would snap one's photo sharing spliffs
with Paul Weller, Joe Strummer, Chrissie Hynde—

but the parcel came back undelivered: no stamp on it—
or got there late, too late for recording—
and once again fame had made a near pass
over Grayson. Near, *nearer*, but yet too distant.

Picaresque Hero

*T*aking (hence?)
indirection to be his friend (cf., Blind Willie McTell:
"I took indirection for to be my friend") and after
some years in the development

of a cogent performance art practice—
with friends, in a basement, in Newcastle—
RG-Bargie, his mind now fully accustomed to dereglement
and in thrall perhaps to some siren Carlton Breweries
    advertisment,
set out for Australia and the impossible
British dream of art in the sun—his intellectual baggage
well stocked with the ballast of *at least three* distinct
paradigms: "All books are crap," (Philip Larkin),
"less is more," (Mies van der Rohe) and something of
the simplicity shared both by Lou's feet and Carl Andre's
"Lever", a line of bricks, which Lou's limbs, protruding as they
    did
on that perhaps one and chance occasion, a little resembled.

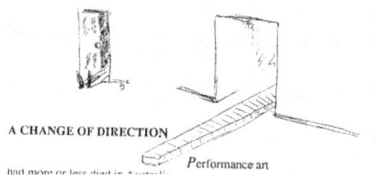

A CHANGE OF DIRECTION

Performance art

A Change Of Direction

Performance art
had more or less died in Australia
when Richard landed—and though he breathed
some lfe into it a blow-up horse
will bear no flogging. Our hero
took up a sort of Post-Conceptual Painting—
pictures of concepts, that had come through the mail, mostly,
whose expression was hard to make clear—fragmentary,
partial, poignant, and often withal pretty (like
the tooled leather of Lou's boots). As with Reed, one might
   wonder

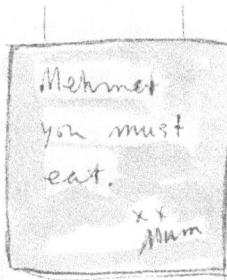

what he reckoned—*though did anyone ask?*—and he could
be supposed to have opinions, *but he was in another*
room—fitting allegory for the way
Richard's texts didn't fit the painting
but bled off the edges
alluding—Lou-Reed-boot-style—to an ur-text
elsewhere, a head that could do the talking. *The*
brilliant thing—as Richard recognised—
best left to the imagination: better than the real letter!
I.e., why wake up Lou? these fragments
of letters, notes, prescriptions—
at once pure presence
and the void of disappointment!

"Back In Five"

*H*is feats! Feat One: one time Richard chiselled "Back in Five"
into a wall—and showed it—in quite large handwriting—
"Very witty"—and, as a day job, moved
into arts administration making sense, reams
and reams of it, for funding bodies, never really overspending
(Feat Two) and (Feat Three) showing 'pretty good shows' the art
    world thought—
between times reading the *NME* for ideas, and in his

last year in the job purchasing (for stability's sake—
after systematic and prolonged dereglement) a bean bag.

One's first view of him, in consequence,
was of the feet—by definition 'pedestrian'
and 'going nowhere', though waggling, in irregular yet happy
    fashion—

as, at the other end, *the thinking* got done: a handsome head
that mused, that quipped, that smiled or grinned, winningly.

With the offer of a drink, telling of a joke, ring
of the phone he has risen, sensible, systematic—
as if a promoter knocked, stepping over the boots, and said
Mr Reed, you're on, or *Hullo, Mr Grayson, fame calling.*

Tho usually it is Suzy, or Alan calling, saying,
We're here already, at the Exeter, getting legless.

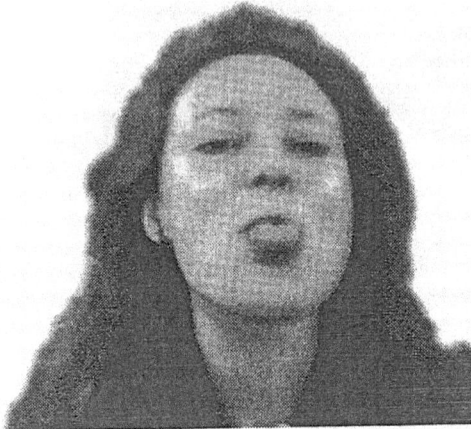

He Did It For Marcel

Later,
seeking to avoid the stigma of 'catering
to the luxury trade' Grayson moved to make his art
of cardboard, giving the rich less for their money
in time honoured fashion: if we live
in the midst of contradiction should't the rich, too,
live in it and, as well, be means tested? Yes, smart on so
many fronts, that Richard. The late works have taken him
to New York—whence real fame beckons—though he
emails still, occasionally, if not regularly, to the E.A.F.
where he is remembered, our brush with greatness
and we would kiss the boots—now departed—of our
    wunderkind.

wunderkind.

(I think of them in a line: the sensible brogues
of Larkin, the Reed boots, and Richard's pumps—at the end of
the sequence, in a style somewhere between theirs—
boots of the foots of greatness.) Where do they walk now,
and where waggle—the galleries and parties of SoHo, its
little bars, fabled Central Park? Do they go skating? And
    Suzy's,
Suzy's too, do they?

uzie's,
too, do they?

As They Come & Korean Mums
Variations For Louise Haselton

drawings in a notebook, the draft of a poem

As They Come

for Anna Banens Kenneally and Louise Haselton

here on this page
a drawing,
vague
& in no way, probably, accurate

tho it gives an idea

the two sculptures —
made, once, on holiday

—thumb-sized,
in plasticine & modelling clay,

a Roman bust—
head, short neck,
indented comma-shapes that suggest tightly curled hair

—& a horse or moose or elk—
it has antlers in the drawing, so not a horse

The Roman's hair ... made with the sharp bit of a
biro cap

                    Head & animal
leaned together.

                              A friendship,
between past
              & present,
6 BC
          & 2007

                    On the island of Hvar.

The figures—*with others*—
                        (members of
toony jazz band
                        —penguin with clarinet,
elephant on saxophone   etc)
                              in blues & purples,
browns & greens—
                    were stood on a balustrade

                                    'the' balustrade
                    #
A view of variegated rooftops
                        the hill that rose behind

                    Sudden, cooling night.
                    #

And in the notebook,
near this drawing,
the draft of the catalogue poem for Louise
with its O'Hara-like beginning
"Today I have $10 in my pocket"

#

Louise's art—
noble & playful

#

works that are
(they have been, they
will be again
next week)
lovely in their otherness,
clear,
eschewing projection
—of depth, the moodily internal—
for something actual:
truths,
of relationship,
gesture, weighted step, reserve,
a kind of dance.
A Louise Haselton
opening, at the E.A.F.

#

'Gone in the legs',

                                        the moose

leans for support

                    on the Roman's head,

                                leans 'into' the head,

                                                        as if

to say, *May I?*

                              #

there for a few days,

                          we made them

one night.

              Gabe, Stace, Anna,

                      Cath & me,

                                Leigh, Yuri.)

Louise's art will be different.

                              Maybe equally evanescent,

as provisional—

                but unsentimental,

                                    immediate.

"'Nietzschean',

            almost,

                    by contrast?"

                                    Ha, ha!

                    # # #

For Louise Haselton

Now when I
walk around this morning
                    I have ten
dollars in my pocket
                    I had more earlier
but as I made my way to work
                    —whistling—
a little, oddly dressed
                    woman
                              asked me
for change & I said yep

        she recognised me
        I recognised her

I am happy for a time & not uninterested
surely something interesting will happen
a new boss a new show to open & another
to write about—Louise's—a pale brilliant
yellow & white
& sculptural pieces that said 'I
am Anthony Caro-meets-A Silly Walk,
but slinky like a Siamese, & ZIPPY
("if you please") like Ornette Coleman' or Thelonius
Monk and Trinkle, Tinkle. "I *said* that,"
said Louise's sculpture—a small piece
that slid across the stage on its
knees & yet, was, 'the while', perfectly still
—but not inert, no—
poised frangipani windmill frond

fond of her, friend?

And a frond   that says Lipchitz, Archipenko,
Florine Stettheimer   Louise Bourgeois

the poem for Louise
could go like that

days ago I had
nothing-to-write today I

face the task.
It is an art I like,

something 'un-alloyed'
about it tho it is

almost literally always
made-up-of-parts what is

un-alloyed is its
sense of impulse a

clarity like a
perfect move a

gift, for us
the world, the

art world comes out
loves it, but has not

the words — it doesn't
need words, nor require them

it is greater than that, it
just is

always with the echo just
of the final move last

step some metal & wood a
bit of shell

a pose held

#

((I remember, in the 90s, work that was difficult))

#

Now

the work seems free, they caper—
or they explain something

by unveiling a fact, a
property we have been

too uptight to admit

sensuous limber amused
— girls —

are they modernist, these Haseltons? they don't
appear to care are they postmodern?

they don't appear to care. They inhabit
a permanent present tense.

Korean Mums

                  My new coffee shop—
I seem to have decided   again
                 to go
for the least popular one.
                  Hipsters run
the more obvious choice
                 With attitude,
that a big crowd buy into,
                so a place
to sit is not easy to find
              The space is small
the queue almost always three at least before
                you

I go instead to a Japanese place
that specializes in waffles
              that
no one buys
          not many
               where there's
never a queue
        and, 'the few who do'
queue briefly.

             Here, to
touch up a review
           A vocabulary thing
aerate it somehow
           Already, here, I've
             used

'briefly'

               my theme, unconsciously? —

nothing ever lasts?

                   Life passes, if you're

an impressionist

        #

(*"Life's always intense* — for a Repo Man")

          #

         here to try that

          #

& to write to Pam

                 "nice poem in *Overland*"

& her friend in it, too,

             I understand

                    —as

I usually don't—

        & like, almost in consequence

Has a month gone by?

My regular appearance

              twice

              a day

Alli & Gina serve

          —Koreans—

they   & the restaurant.

           Not Japanese.

               I've

                 written

the review.

        Cath's been away.

Read numerous books.

Stoner,

a book on Braque,   Carrie Tiffany
(her first)

#

Bassani's

The Smell Of Hay

was good.

(Tho Stoner — I 'needn't have bothered')

Carrie is good   (tho less
focused than her 'birds' book)

& Bapo,

Nick's new one

Write

the poem for Louise

—for Louise's show—

#

— "Louise Haselton"
OPENING

at the EAF, October

sixteenth —

#

(the week after : the launch of Aneta's book)

#

(From some travel notes—)

we were eating, about fourteen

                                                              of us
on Lumbarda,

              a vast long table   on a
                           balcony
(overlooking trees, garden, the sea

                           the Adriatic)

                      a 'set-piece',
from a European movie.

                         I had to announce
                  … that I had been stung by a
                                bee,
on the tongue — I didn't expect to die
                                           etc etc
              Still, 'there you are' — 'now you know'
                           ("No regrets.
                         I think you all
are very nice people
                       always have. Ha ha.")
                                etc.

in fact this stuff
is left out of my diary (!)

tho I always remember it

                           as I do
              Ivan Perniketty
                         —similarly unrecorded,
                           & similarly remembered—

                                        a tiny flyer
                                          for him
lives among the bric-a-brac in my writing room.

A4 posters were everywhere on the island
advertising Ivan's concert. A piano recital
that we all thought we might go to—why not?—

                    •

weeks later I do a drawing,
of the thumb-sized head I sculpted, on Hvar.

                        The others
made cartoon animals, playing
instruments—hippo-with-bongo, pelican-with-
clarinet sort of thing,
                            in various colours

We laughed & drank.
                        A hot early night,
                        that cooled

                        — September
2007 —

    We left them out overnight,

& next day I saw that the mule or moose, or
whatever it was Anna made—
had wilted a little
—'gone in the legs'—& now leaned,

comforted, friendly, against
'my' small, antique head.

As if

to enquire, May I?
Is this alright?

(Hanna Barbera

meets History)

I write it down

& tack it

to Louise's poem,

.

the small figures, generally, had had
the same off-balance grace
her things have

#

(tho the Haselton show:

'almost gone'—

in another week it will come down)

#

in

my Korean coffee shop
in Adelaide

late morning
November,

reading

Blaise Cendrars

Who,

someone says 'gave himself to the street'

the street I inhabit *for a moment every day*—

The dream
of *life*—which I suppose it is

(I'm not a hunter-gatherer running thru a forest,
a courtesan in 14th-century Japan, a soldier
smoking a cigarette, holding his gun, eyes alert
in Syria or Iran …
              & I'm 'going to work', it's
about that time—unlock the doors, bring in
the bins, turn the computer on, email Pam).

Ivan Pernicki is the correct spelling: he was to perform Matz, Bartok, Pejacevic,
Rachmaninov, Debussy and Liszt, says the flyer. And 'Korean Mums'—(the
title of a Schuyler poem)—are flowers—"Mums" being a contraction from
"Chrysanthemums". Gina & Alli should not be compared to flowers—too
modern—& calling them "mums" makes me smile, but they are young, I like
them. And 'Japanese'? I was wrong, Korean.

Little Elegy, 1984

I shudder while feeling quite happy—
I have just read a Ted Berrigan poem,

while I have seen a jar of *Cow* gum
look 'clean' but 'sickening'.

At the same time.

You can do this when you're stoned.
And now, the cat gets back,

to my lap,
from the table,

as I had told it it would—
just a while ago.

The radio's going & has just explained
that the bassoon is only 'good' for 'Satire' & 'Mourning'.

And there's a lot of
slow mourning on,

& has been for some time.

(I don't mind.
The cat doesn't seem to care either.

The cat I think prefers mourning ... to satire.
"I'll do the satire around here ...

(if anyone's going to do satire)"
is her attitude. *"This's good,"* she adds.)

I'd like to have 'just met' Ted Berrigan
& got along with him.

I've been in mourning, for him—
ever since I found out he'd died.

#

Quite a while ago now.

#

It changes the poems somehow, a little.
It's true:

something I guess mournful is happening,
I can't do anything about it.

Myles Ahead

Listless, 'happy',
then affectless

—& hip—

anxious then
about hipness

then affecting not
to care.

Nothing
of great moment. So,

a kind of cool,
then 'love'—a claim

made for it, the
'fact' of it asserted

A parade before the reader—
of self sufficiency

i. e.,

"these notes are
for myself (do you

wish that you could
be like that?

I *am.*)" She
was good once—

& not unlike.

'Star Eyes'

I do all the
usual things—

(& am, to
that extent,
a caricature)—

'Star Eyes'
then 'Social Call'
playing,

read Schuyler
'This Dark Apartment'—
waiting on this

new poem. Yesterday
I read, quickly, a
bio of Lou Reed

quickly written, too
(the familiar facts
surface again)

email Pam, Laurie.
Laurie's advice:
remain calm

be yourself.
*How is that
going to work!?*

Send Pam
images for putative
board game

'Boogie In Front'
(Big Jay McNeely)
next.

The studio quiet.
Rain I can hear, falling,
on the grape vine,

Cath & Yuri's voices
murmuring next door
('Tondelayo'—I wonder

if I will drop this one,
when it comes to
typing up?) Day

two after Xmas
almost cool (maybe
in fact cool)

after the 40 degrees
of the big day. 'Little
By Little' now

a live version. I
recently saw
footage of him—

Junior Wells—

34 years ago
come, with
Buddy Guy to

impose himself on
the stage, succeeding
then backing off

cool again while
Guy ploughs on.
'Footprints', then

'Gingerbread Boy'
Where, asks Cath
are our hammers?

I show her.
Chooks to be fed.
I feed them.

Poem, how are you going?

The poem that ends
on a question. Like,
you come in the studio—

face a new canvas,
make some scribbles on it
some smudge, some scrawl

—(What, you're *Cy Twombly* now ?!?!?)—

At any rate the
'canvas' is besmirched—no longer
calling out—& you wander off,

time to kill.

Tho I like time (I'm
'in my element'—
but to what end?

Little Walter
Magic Sam, Art
Blakey, coming up)

Briefing Mary Christie

Dear Mary,

It's Sunday morning & I'm sitting in the brightest corner
of our big back room—with coffee & a few handfuls of
roasted almonds, & dates—
                          after copious slices of bread
and a few oranges & a bit of a read about the Ou Li Po.
Well, I've washed clothes
                          & put them out,
                                        weeded a bit,
played with the dog,
                    done the dishes.
                                   Just in case
you think I'm still the feckless layabout
                          of Westbury Street days.
And I'm listening
                to a CD I made
                             especially for
the first half hour
                  of the Lee Marvin Readings.
                          I open the doors at 7.30
                                   press play
& at about 5 minutes to 8 the short 'I Spy' theme comes on
                                        which always
amuses me
         & signals that I should stop serving drinks &
chatting with potential customers,
                          briefing the nervous new readers etc
& should
       hide the money,

                              turn the airconditioning or heater off
the sound on
                    & start the show running. I'm usually ready to go
just as the last tune ends.

                    ('You're My Thrill' — Pepper Adams)

India?
          Mary, Yes, we would like to come.

When, but?
                    The literary festival
—at Jaipur?
                    (I can't see that my work would have much appeal in India.
I suppose I could regard that
                              as their problem,
                                        if they give me the ticket.)

Milli sent the photo of her & Seb—
with Hector at their feet (in a stroller).
I have it where I can see it. They look
so great
          & it reminds me of them
& their up-for-it energy.
                    (Both of them
rather glamorous.)
                    Milli's letter
took up—& finished—
the handwritten *beginning*
of the letter you had emailed me,

filling it with her news.
                    (So I'll email

them a copy of this. "Dear Mary, & Mill,
et tu, Seb, you handsome brute"
                                        etc)
(that would be good manners)

"I'm up to Sydney to read with Pam—in
early September, Tuesday night, the 9th,
at Sappho's in Glebe, Mill, if you're free
& in the mood,
                    & Seb, if you're back
from wildest Africa—"
                        to read & also
to see Sal, whose
kidney transplant
has gone well. I think
the early adjustments
& monitoring
of how it's running
& of drug side-effects
will still be going on.
                    I've been reading very closely
a novel of hers in draft form—about life
in the hospital on dialysis
                        interspersed,
every second chapter,
                    with a Sei Shonagon-style
Japanese court melodrama.
The stories parallel each other
& both are very detailedly pictured.
                            It's good—
better than anything
she's done before.
I hope she still has plenty of time.

(An old girlfriend, Seb, Mill.)

Kurt is in Berlin—
after weeks in London
and a month or so a few weeks prior,
showing art, & making art, in New York.
He might not need much encouragement
to come to India.
If you're interested. I'm not sure
of his agenda.

       A pizza party last week—our first
for a few years—a Sunday arvo:
for Louise Haselton, Jenni
Robertson & daughters —
& half a dozen other people.

We'll do a bigger one soon.

Louise seems well. Though she did say
that she teaches Monday & Tuesday
& then spends most of Wednesday
in bed & doesn't do Thursday or Friday.
Should improve after three or four
more months. Jenni is well,
                worried
about what the aggression
of high school students
says about the country. Her daughters were lovely:
they played with the dog,
read books, did a bit of hide-&-seek.

Work's good. Our next show

might be alright, actually. The artist
usually looks to me
like he has ripped off
someone else local, & thinks
no one will notice. As in,
Gee, I could've made that. It would
suit *me, & reflect well on me too*—

& so he stands by a newly-made
Craige Andrae or Shaun Kirby—

like someone getting their photo taken
in front of a painted scene: he pretends

to be the hunter, puts the pith helmet on
& his foot on the bear's head,

the photographer bends down
to the lens. Poof! The powdered flash
goes off & it's done.

This show doesn't look *original*—a bit of
Melbourne's Guy Stuart & a bit
of George Popperwell maybe—
but it looks pretty good. A
different bear than theirs.

Anna P had a large show at AGSA,

some of it impressive. But
generally you think, *I didn't know*

people knew how to do *this anymore*—

on the other hand, I can see why they might have stopped!

Gerome meets Freudian, Victorian-era Surrealism.)
Better

was a Stewart MacFarlane show
at Central Gallery. He's gotten to be very good.

Tho as Laurie said
'Nipple-factor eleven!'

The year seems to be
racing by: but you'll get
this letter (well, it's an
email, isn't it!) before you
get on the plane again.

    Cath & I
might be going to see Gabe
in London over January.

(*Here's lookin' at yer!* "Here's looking
up your old address," as you used to say

when we first met.)

That brings you up to date, Maz.

    Ken

"Hi, Small Bug!"

"Hi, small bug, I'm not grass—but climb me. It's
me, by the way, Issa!"

That sort of thing.
                    How many bugs have I dealt with
down here?
                    A few spiders
                            I've killed.
                                    A scorpion,

                                                    &

an insect
          I've *helped move*
                      —from the sliding door
                                  frame
to outside—
                the cement step, the garden.

I have spent a lot of time
                      perusing the *poster*
—*BUGS OF OUR TIME ?* —

                      flightless insects,
primitive-winged insects, water insects etcetera
their fanciful names:
                      chalcyd wasp,
                                        water penny,
the true midge
                (a false midge, by implication, exists—
                            the pseudo midge ?)

\#

My oldest friends, a meeting after forty years—
how will it go, how *might* it go?

                                  Or, since it will
—we meet on Sunday—

                        it will, but how?

\#

                                 Ichneumon wasp

damsel fly

the (plain) water beetle
whose rummy cheerful

look I like

the emperor (or 'gum') moth

& I think "Gotha"—
a German aeroplane?—
"Genghis"—a conqueror?

\#

I read some more Patrick Leigh Fermor

\#

An exhausting day
of driving up & down the coast,

we do in fact rise suddenly & say
"We have to go!" tho our hosts

are not startled

familiar with the concept "the last ferry":

#

I consider these bugs again,

                              as I am
'here', again, now.

                         They *can* read
as a lesson, an illustration—
of orders, & kinds of life

(different 'stations' etc)

                         Leigh Fermor
mentions "mooch" & I wonder

when "mooching about" became
a regularly used phrase.
                                        'Moose the
Mooche' I think at the same time.

         But I am not mooching—

This is a small house.
I sit

—very still—

by the sliding door, in the light

—fly-screen between me & the green outside …
… where the real bugs are

a moment later I test that phrase,
hear it in Penny's voice,

see Alex glance outside, smile.
As I would smile if Penny said it.

Two Poems For Viv Miller

A Picture Of Our Times

A new exercise book—especially for the
poem Viv wants. But in the coffee shop
I have already begun, my left hand
clutching, I note (what makes me notice
this?) my glasses case—well, it is
under my hand, merely; my elbow (I wear
    a leather jacket, I note, further, or 'again')
rests on the table, my right holds the pen; the Journal
    of Eugene Delacroix, just begun, what a treat
    lies in store (I hope); a coffee on its serviette,
    on a plate; plastic bags with new pads & pens.
Everybody in the shop talks. Not Art—it's the arts
    'industry' talking. Grants. The street goes by,

outside, like goldfish, people, cars
floating past in silence—a world I cannot hear:

vans park, move off, silently, an African woman
in a long dress of green passes, in a
very different head-space, probably, than mine—
(space in which I realise I'm using the *old* pad,
    not the notebook)—our two head-spaces—
    like maps of our world, transparencies
    that might overlay each other, to produce
    a truth. It's very complex? But real enough.

A Picture In Our Hall

An old picture of Viv Miller's—an 'early
picture', now that Viv has moved on, gotten
    older herself, while remaining, of course, young—
    lives currently
in our hall. Where I like it. But I liked it best
claiming its spot—where you saw it as you passed
    by the doorway—in
the bedroom, where it hung to the left of the bed,
unheimlich & homely, 'both'—&
reminded me of the sort of art used in 50s films—
essential but unsubtle—often very funny—*clues,*
    signifiers,

of modernity, complexity, of a
fatal flaw in a character ... or as decoration
    in a psychiatrist's office:

vicious, overly complex, neurotic—too intellectualised
    (overly intelligent? *Too smart for* his/her *own good?*)—
intellectual modern life. Viz., Herbert Lom, a
Viennese psychoanalyst, in a tv show
seemingly only I watched, late at nights, as a
    kid. Or the picture is a sight-gag, indicating
    these same things—in a Hitchcock movie.
    But which, *The Trouble With Harry? North
    By Northwest?* Indicating *the same things*
    but with irony. It's 'abstract', Vivien's picture,

but with a curly, grub-like shape that winks at one
from the painting & reminds of 'Swee'Pea', the
baby in *Popeye*. It crawls inch-worm style
within the space of the painting, cute, nutty,
innocent & perverse. It is very complex.

A Travelin' Man

all afternoon in a car
parked at the ferry wharf
— Pam Brown

At the beginning of Laurie's *Crab & Winkle*
the quote, I note, is the *Shangri-las*

the word "*rumori*"
is in there too

faint echoes of Australia
as he begins to settle in
begins determinedly

(their possessions   as Laurie says
—their "worldly goods"—
"still somewhere in the Indian ocean")

He & Rosemary,
landed in Kent,
Canterbury

where Rosemary
will take up her job, in law, professoring

So Sasha, Denis
Pam & I,
Alan, others,
ghost in & out of the early
pages

163

Laurie still half in Australia

Australia, functioning maybe, as a reference point, a measure

('imperial',

the empire come back   *to verify things*

via

pop songs

via sensible or far-fetched ambitions

(Sasha)—

till Laurie, I expect

—till Laurie as *he*

must expect or anticipate—

begins to feel

on-the-pace

less foreign

'here'   ('Here'?)

("Here" being "there",

(Kent)   (England)   (London)

as

he will & did

#

as he would & has?

#

Published now eight years

—the record of a year settling in (some time spent

setting & designing)—

     Crab & Winkle must have been written

ten or more years ago

        now he might allow

    his mind to drift south again, as they

prepare to leave

      for Sydney, I think

          —tho

            a year

or two away.

     Here he'll miss them, might be

missing them now already

       the mind, as it will,

ahead of itself.

      Mine always is.

         Who can live

'in the moment'?

    #

   Not me.

     "No time!" ha ha ha

    #

I'm reading

    for the first time

       Under Western Eyes

no I'm not—I'm reading *Heart Of Darkness*

    #

the early pages   set   maybe   close to Kent

                      evocative

                               of

a serene mildness

                #

                  & Johnson's *Lives Of The Poets*

which is amusing

          & intelligent

                    (tho who needs me

to remark it?)

            some of the lives & their passions

reminding of literary figures still current

                  maybe

'perennial' these acts & motivations

                  —& Tim Wright's

small collection

            lines & phrases in it that I love

am drawn to

        that I can maybe   draw heat *from*

        I am situated

            in or

            between

Laurie's last decade

        Conrad's what? 1890s?

  Tim

(in Melbourne, *now* more or less)

                        Pam Brown

                                        & me & Cath

(—'now' definitely—& currently on Bruny Island),

& Johnson's eighteenth century & sure, generalising, imperial
latinity & secure English good sense

                              (*Get the picture?*)

                                        (to quote

            Laurie Duggan
                  &
            'Shadow' Morton)

Sasha
        —the editor, & sole writer, of *The Only Sensible News*—

whose project was the resurrection of Harry Hooton

And now a younger friend of Pam's

                        —Pam was closer
than us to Sasha—

                  has gone in to bat for him. Harry Hooton.

I thought Hooton was an awful poet.

                        Which I told Sasha.

            #

                  timor mortis conturbat me,

                        Laurie quotes,

recalling John Forbes

occasioned by
a *HIGH VOLTAGE* warning
Laurie sees
on the side of a generator.

Thinking, I suppose, Here I am in England,
where John went before me
the strangeness of it

#

Will this
continue, as a line by line commentary on Laurie's poem?

Not the worst thing one could do.

#

Tho I'd soon
catch him up
—he already having done the hard thinking—

the heavy lifting,
in John's phrase

& then where would I be?

here?
there?

"footsteps in the courtyard
the rattle of leaves on the path"

              (Womack & Womack)

"In the offing the sea & sky
welded together without a joint"

        &

"A haze rested on the low shores
that ran out to sea in vanishing flatness"

"What greatness had not floated on the ebb
of that river into the mystery of 'an unknown earth'!"

        & so on

Hmm, I should quote Sam & Tim

       & perhaps I will

inevitable?

      irresistible?

        a bad idea?

           (but
           'none the less'?)

at the cafe past the turn-off to Adventure Bay

on the way to Alonnah

                                with Cath

                                                she reading
                                                Zadie Smith

which I'll read after her
                        I read *Crab & Winkle.*

                                                                At
first
        —for a moment— the shop seems too crowded:
tourists—New Zealanders, Aussies, some Singaporeans

                                                        the owner very
                                                        talkative

so it is *very* noisy.

                                But where else to go
                                on an island?

                                                        So we
                                                        stay

there is somewhere else to go because the crowd moves on
& we sit & read   & write   exchange remarks

                                                        then 'go'—

to buy petrol, groceries, have a walk on the beach

'Adventure Bay'

— tho the bay, the beach, live up to it —
the automatic thought: what can Cook & Co have made of it
all those years ago?

idyllic?

the berry farm is shut
contrary to its advertisement

pale blue, silvery, the sands
white as I have ever seen them

our prints the first today,
aside from those of a dog

& numerous small birds

#

two plovers, a dotterel
a pacific gull (a 'dominican')

#

see Ian & Lorraine in the afternoon
see Dan & Sophie that night

Three days later, a trip to Adventure Bay, again for groceries—

a trip for promised meals, with Ian & Lorraine, & Pat & Chris
the next few days.

"No nice milk,"
so Cath rings Lorraine (just, at that moment, at the checkout in
Kingston). Lorraine will bring us some tonight.

A walk
on the beach near the berry farm ("closed till October")

tourists photographing each other on the rocks before the
swell of incoming waves & the enormous panorama—
that says 'Endless space', 'time' & 'miles away'. Cath goes
for a skinny dip at the other end, the water invigorating
& cold. Small puffins & large gulls gathered near by,
keeping thirty metres' distance from us as we move down
the beach. Cath has seen the eagle this morning, a sea
eagle, perched in a large tree in the neighbour's yard. I
see it too. (Gabe's idea of Cath's motto— *"I've seen an
eagle"* & *"I'm going in"*—proved true.)

I take some photos for Cath. They resemble Richard
Hamilton's of Marilyn—tho of course the special virtue
of those was to have her resemble every woman In That
Same Situation: full of enjoyment, endorsed, &
communicating these things, their smile addressed not
to the camera but the person behind it. These photos
verify that Cath did, in fact, go in.

Zadie Smith. I finish *Heart Of Darkness*: a mess finally.
As Conrad must surely have known. I haven't read much
of him for forty years now, except for *The Nigger Of The
Narcissus* a year or two back. Also impossible. (Should

I read more? *Nostromo? Lord Jim?*)

For now, tho,
Zadie, *The Autograph Man.* Three years back I read
NW & liked it very much.

We go home, rest & cook.

Lorraine & Ian show up early—after an exhausting day
on the mainland, seeing to various things. They have
disinterred, from years in storage, a standard lamp that
we can use. They leave. (No dinner tonight.) And we
go squidding at Lunawanna—return for late tea.

#

Once or twice a day the phone pings, telling us of photos
arriving, of the grandchildren in Adelaide—Noah mooning
in the parking lot of Marion shopping centre, Gabe looking
on, Max, a small general or fearless merchant banker—a
'commando' merchant banker perhaps—short videos of him
learning words from Anna. Say "garden," Max. Max, say
"cat".

I must remember that I want to end with Tim's "I move thru
the traffic like a pin."

Tho, why do I
like it?—Tho I know I do.

#

Pat & Chris for a day or two, then the drive back with them—
ferry (abjure cheese shop—no time!) & prep for dinner that
night at their place, Olga & Paul coming.

#

We go on an amusing op-shop crawl, with Chris, the next day.
Pat stays home to prepare his Spanish for an end-of-day
weekly tutorial.

Chris phones from just up the street—she has gone for
vegetables—telling us to come out & see the spectacular sky.
We set off with Pat in the lead, see the fabulous sky—whorls
of red Altdorfery clouds against beautiful bruised, plum-blue
background cloud, & patches of silver & moonstone-grey. Call
into Betts Gallery on the way back & see the paintings there. A
designer's take on the possibilities of various modes of
representation, contrasted together: scumbled expressionist paint
used representationally over mirror-enamel surfaces & offset
against geometric abstraction, bits of stencilled nineteenth-century
drawing or cartoon. Salle-meets-Patrick Caulfield-meets-
Gordon Bennett, pop art & Rauschenberg distantly behind.
His earlier work reminded of Stephen Bram schooled on (Kenneth)
Noland.

#

"I glide thru the traffic like a pin"

Peregian

A kind
of *tristesse*
attends reading
Jimmy Schuyler—
the melancholy
of many of his
poems, the
knowledge
you will never
write like him—
& if you did
what would
be the point,
they would still
be his:
            the bleak,
sad days—that
belonged to him—of
grey, &
blue;
            cloud; inter-
mittent light; some
found, small blooms
—& happiness
drawn from them;

the completed poem.

Anyway, here
I am, observing

rounded grey-white 'dots'
—minuscule—
lodged
between the
bricks of the
paving—too small
to be confetti, too small
to be packaging,
hard when I
pick one up. I
drink my coffee.
CIBOS, Gouger Street.
A Wednesday morning.
(I have no watch
so I spare you
that detail.) April.
         I write a poem
about Max—
whose small fingers
will grab my face, my ears,
nose—grab my
shirtfront—they did
at Peregian beach—
& pull me close: a
small unblemished gangster
or mogul ("Listen
to me, Pal") We were
on the balcony—
among the palms—above
the pool below.
Good times.

4
Wiesengrund

Wiesengrund

for César Aira and Theodor Adorno

So here I am,

           Adorno in hand

                   It's

going to be a tough day

                Ready, in case.

And a list building, of things to do

               (Make a copy

—not just by hand—of the passages from Aira

Reflecting

       his agreement, with Donald Brook,

                     and me,

& Clement Greenberg

              and Thomas—that 'individual

talent'—Stearns Eliot)

          In a cafe

alone,

       if you don't count Adorno

                 or John

Levy

       whom I mean to address.

           "Hullo, John."

"I think we can all agree——to disagree"

                                                I say to the

bunch,

                since we always did.

                                        And they

                                          relax

No longer expectant

                      and look   in different directions

Donald looks

                 out the corner of his eye

at Adorno

                Clement wanders outside,

                                spits,

lights a cigar

                Eliot greens

& fades away

                  bilious? 'Cheshire cat"?

                                                      I,

                ——in a tutorial

                1970——

Donald: "You are not going to defend

       the Expression Theory, are you?"

                              "Yes. I think

                                 I am"

                my reply.

And with a panoply of epicycles,

                          demurrals, riders

—& acknowledgement

               that 'all is reading' and

                        'learned response'—

                               have,

maybe.

          Tho could you call that 'consistently'?

John's poems might be *apropos*

                   and a 'test case'

          because tact might be their

                     greatest

                     asset

Tact that is his

             —not even a strategy

(an ethic ?

          a private code)

                  reticence

invisibly in play with FULL DISCLOSURE
& invention

The poems allow us to bring feeling to them—

washes and touches of colour, that the pictures
drawn allow —'elicit'?— *support* anyway.

WAS MARQUET AN EXPRESSIONIST ?

                                        I think you see
                                        my point.

Ha ha.
        "But anyway" !
                                (a turn of
phrase
            rhetorical move
                    tactical move
                                            it
can't be solely Australian, can it?)

                                (Beginning a
poem with "so"
                    :
                    an own goal) …

                                        Greenberg
is going to stomp back in—
                            "So let's see these
                            poems,"
—or maybe, true to form—
                            "You stink!"
and punch me.
            "Punch Donald," I say,
                                        "I never
abandoned you!
                    Entirely."
                                        Men
are so full of shit.

I watch the handsome
dude, young,
address a table of women & 'graciously'
take his leave
Of course, what should he do?

Be graceless?

#

—Too blandly confident: a gift to the ladies—

#

The gender balance
is all wrong here—I introduce
Pam Brown, Lucy Lippard
a few of whose
'remarks'
—the merest phrases—
have been touchstones

"visual muzak" (for Jules Olitski),
"the cult of
the direct and the difficult"
Reliable
for firmness, position
& where's Laurie
(to
ruin the gender balance again) ?
#
Poems "that
look too much like poetry now

may look a lot less like it in the future"

[Laurie Duggan]
#
which returns me to Aira

on 'Creation' versus

'mere production',

and *Most art*

(it being the latter)

as 'craft'.

That distinction. (Hullo, Donald.)

Or '*as kitsch*', I offer Greenberg,

at that moment

grinding his cigar underfoot

He stands and looks out at a bus

that passes us

outside the Middle Store coffee shop.

The bus stops

& off gets Rosalind Krauss

Very swish clothing

An art-world princess

"from New York"

or, by now, dowager warrior.

#

Greenberg —(I look)— has disappeared

A small

Cheshire cat smells the remains of his cigar

#

This poem

shows no tact

tactless

Except where

grace might be particularly required

or out of cowardice.

Yes, it's true—*this* is the self with whom I
'must abide' —

ME

(*"I'll get that—*

I *pay the bills"*),

And this bozo here

—who thinks

(holds the pen)—

. . .

("I pay the bills")

John —

John's new book—

could teach a few lessons

that I'll probably never learn

"... tact as the saving accommodation between alienated human beings ... seemed to him [Goethe] inseparable from renunciation, the relinquishment of total contact, passion, unalloyed happiness. ... *But what has happened since* makes Goethean renunciation look like fulfilment. Tact and humanity—for him the same thing—have in the meantime gone exactly the way *from which they were to save us.* For tact, we now know, has its precise historical hour. Now it lives on only in the parody of forms, and in arbitrarily devised or recollected etiquette for the ignorant, of the kind preached by unsolicited advisers in newspapers—while the basis of agreement that *carried* those conventions has given way to the blind conformity of car-owners and radio-listeners. ... Other than convention there was nothing by which tact could be measured.

...

The question as to someone's health, required by and expected by upbringing, becomes inquisitive or injurious; silence on sensitive subjects empty indifference—as soon as there is no rule to indicate what is and what is not to be discussed. Thus individuals begin, not without reason, to react antagonistically to tact: a certain kind of politeness, for example, gives them less the feeling of being addressed as human beings, than an inkling of their inhuman conditions, and the polite run the risk of seeming impolite by continuing to exercise politeness."

pages 36—37, *Minima Moralia*, 'On the dialectic of tact'

I played with the word 'tact' last
night, reading Levy's book

SILENCE LIKE
ANOTHER NAME

toyed with using it in my commentary.

To open up—today—on this page in Adorno is surprising.

#

I expect to find
how ('exactly') dated
this makes me

#

But I always find the
Negative Verdict
of an earlier age
chastening
Salient, valuable
to exactly the degree
it is chastening
Hold that bus, conductor!
Chase that train, Coltrane! etcetera.

I change the subject.

"Anyway!"
(a kind of
sigh
the ellipses stretching out
from the phrase,

an atoll, a diaspora, a line of Pacific islands

Where to now?

2

[Near Shepherdess Walk, and Adrian's, Chiswick]

Across the way the kids play & I watch them.
On the roof, down a level & two levels further—
chasings, desultory cycling, one pretends
to shoot people—*the others*—'pretends'—
I mean, he does but a toy gun that
can do no physical harm. Our building—taller,
so I can see them … or look

at the sky: London's many shades of grey
the softnesses of clouds, the
buildings in the distance; a
mostly low horizon line of dark
(the odd very new build with colour in it)
reflecting late afternoon sun.
•

oyster
moonstone
dove grey
flecks & hints
of mackerel, pitch
•

The sound is the key—I can hardly hear them,
the occasional shout,
the pellet he shoots, one time, goes clack against a door

\#

I pass & look in
& see Cath asleep on the bed—

a horizontal—echoed above
by wall, window—the framing *de stijl*

of the iron, & the colour of the frame:
sky, curtains, screen partially drawn

It reminds me of a like scene
more than twenty years ago,
a wondrous room—the Hotel Andrea.
Florence, 1997.
Umbrous—creams—& biscuit tans—
a soft dark room, generous proportions.

We're in Allan & Linda's temporary flat.
Temporarily.
Small. But canny, hip, efficient design.
London 2019.
     We're 'old' ...

Tho not dying—not any more
than anybody else is. The kids opposite are living tho—

faster than us. Collaborating, cooperating, laughing,
        shooting & hiding,
the human stuff.

\#

I read Kleinzahler who is worrying
about death a lot
Well, who isn't? Ken, Ken
the young they don't worry

Life, this
is Augie's
            'getting the best of it'—

flavours
            smells,
                        sounds, mostly—
& scenes

            And a melancholy that
attaches & he refuses

So a rueful beauty glows,
a nimbus around each vignette—

as trucks roar by
stirring dust & chemicals,

a stiffening the character needed.

                        "August,
have I got it right?"

#

A young woman passes the
window of my coffee shop
—Artisan—
hair a frosted silver pink I'm sure
not currently fashionable. Tho just right.
She is beautiful.
Gone in seconds—I will
remember her, now —will I ?— remember

the fact of her—
because I've written. Someone else
will remember *exactly* how beautiful—
pale, pale, pale—
as they do in England

#

Kleinzahler: slightly bluff,
concerned to be authoritative—

but why not—should he be
uncertain, indecisive?

#

An old lady ('little'—the
full complement—but tough
in dark brown weather gear)

rides her bicycle
gestures remonstratively
to a motorist

—a beemer—
who has not given way

as she rides on, a moderate pace,
& is gone too

#

A very tiny, slightly older

woman I nursed when I was
young. A nursing home:
I would regularly fall asleep
—two long, back-to-back weekend shifts—
in the first lecture Monday

The guy who explained the Baroque
mystified, that this happened
every week. He gave me
high marks. I never came
to tutes, he never knew my
name, tho I knew his, once.
Of couse I did. I mean
I knew it, even, ten years ago.
German, a crazy accent I
still remember "per-soock-er-

logical." Small older women
their fierceness, fragility.

His name. Hers, I think, was Maudie

#

Durer's mother
   —not quite so old, so gnarled

I see her appear left
   shake her hand, reprovingly,

at a motorist

        who fails

to give way.

She pedals on,
on the footpath, her hand held up tellingly—

in the right

The beemer goes past
& out of the picture

'Beemer'—
do they use that term here?

&, as I'm in London,
must I use their terminology?—
A BMW
She rides on,
a moderate pace
calm
remonstration made.

•

Maudie: carolling, light,
bird-like conversation, wordless

Her very tight grip

3

WIESENGRUND AGAIN

[AXAT and LONDON]

Fluted tones ('birdlike') rise & fall

Richard cooks
                                        a complicated but
promising dish

                        Suzy moves around
rearranging the kitchen,
things are put away — we read,
guests, a little guiltily 'off duty'

Emails I send to Anna
                                        images
of today's journey — French towns
their windows shuttered, their
pleasantly-coloured facades, trees,

a picture of us all at a table in a square
with some expatriates

            #

The radio—the 'fluted tones'—
provides comforting filler
for this quiet time
                        of 'work'

                                              an inane
Lord Peter Whimsey

                                 first broadcast in 1959
the accents showily civilized

London, when we get home to Chiswick
is hard work — but livelier.
                                    Beautiful at
dusk & at night
                        The Chiswick shops lit up, the
streetlights,
                 the trees, the traffic
                                     High-ceilinged rooms
of restaurants
                         brightly lit,
enshrine those dining, advertise their
enclosing, caring, privileging function

                        The Thames is high,
& coming away from the Carpenter's Arms
we find a street partially flooded. An
expensive car attempts to pass thinks better & reverses.

A beautiful girl on the train who has ruined her face
with subtle but too overall surgery: she keeps her face
covered with her cap's visor, attends to her dog, a
white French bulldog. Her clothes—leggings,
expensive trainers, a funky cotton or denim jacket—
very stylish. She looks up & her face is alien,
'beautiful' but frightening. She looks down, attends

to her dog.

Amongst the hipsters, & ordinary workers, customers
I watch a man—seventy?—in cardigan, T-shirt, rumpled
cargo pants—attend closely to the columned figures
of the financial pages, occasionally he marks things
with his pen. He finishes his coffee up & lights
a cigar, finances done, sets off.

The girl at Artisan has a fabulous, scornful pout, lips
in dark red, dark hair tied back & up: she does the job
well, is good with customers, in repose her face says,
How many more years will I have to serve shitty coffee
to shitty customers before I can go back to Poland?

As we walk Suzy produces a squeaking, high-pitched toot
through a plastic straw—funny—mosquito-like—but it is a
reparative vocal exercise, she says. She does some
histrionic Edith Piaf song and an old man, at the
rural French market we are walking through, applauds
as he passes. Then a devilish 'Tomorrow Belongs To Me'.
No takers. I get her to try the theme from *The Untouchables*
(Eliot Ness) & *The Perry Mason Show*. Everything—*any*thing—
sounds amazing. 'I See The Bad Moon Rising'.

The Carpenter's Arms, out the back, where a woman
tells us of her mother's teenage love of 'Sydney-in-the-sixties'—
her dream of going back there. Her father's making
'the most expensive' (the longest ever) 'phonecall of his life'—
so as to persuade her to return & marry him

Lars en Vercors where the Jewish kids were protected in WWII
                              (under the Italians, who—at least
                              until the fall of Mussolini—
                              administered
                              that part of occupied France)

        #
Perec was there.
        #

Richard's taste in music
                              —songs,
chosen, valued—always, I think—for the significance
of the lyrics
                    their aptness to the age   David Bowie
Johnny Cash
                              where *I* go
                                        typically
                                        shamefully?—
for expression

                    My ludicrous suggestion

                    'No One Knows'
                    by Dion

(the Italian
          —'Italian-American'—
                              softness)

& Adorno

———

also Italian

(a little)

What?! I hear the world protesting

Well, German

then

WHAT ?!

"Well, for a while there I thought

I *was*,"

'for a little bit,'

says Adorno 'ruefully',

joking.

Jewish

The desire to wear

two hats

Or design the new, 'composite' headgear

#

What am I?

#

What kind of man are you?

ask the Raelettes

Jewish, I sometimes think?

No I don't.
Western, I guess,
culturally.
An atheist, an
'Australian' —
who writes quietly in a
restaurant

Anglo sort-of

if Adorno says, 'It's all shit' (not to
quote him directly: a paraphrase) who's

to disagree ?

"For this I fight!" I say
(a joke I haven't tried in a long time) —

& to Adorno — "are
you with me?"
Ha ha.
He gets up from
the table
pushes back his chair
grabs a weapon (a
fork
!)
& we exit onto Winston Avenue
(the Winston Avenue
of 'the Mind'?)

to solve this problem.

('to mess up a hair of the night' ?)

to solve every problem.

I look to Abstract Painting —

"Abstract Painting,

can you help?"

Lucy Lippard, "Maybe.

I think not."

"Christopher Wool?

can *he*?"

"I doubt it."

Suzy's art, Richard's, might be more to

the point.

Poetry?

"Just maybe" — Patti Smith.

Pam Brown: "I doubt it. I'd like it to—
but I doubt it."

Rosalind Krauss

says nothing,

has ordered an affogato.

Tough.

John, where do I go from here?

#

An expensive car
attempts to pass thinks better & reverses. Why

are we here? In fact to see all this—
life, normalcy, 'conditions elsewhere'—
to return & live our own.
The many, very various, faces of London.
Wendy tomorrow, for tea or lunch, & then we are in the air.

NOTES

Birds of Rome—incorporates excerpts from Charles North's 'A Note on Labor Day', published in his book *The Year of the Olive Oil.*

"Hullo! (Yours Cordially)"—takes off from Ron Padgett's poem, 'A Brief Correspondence Course'—in which he imagines ending "Yours cordially" (while in fact he is *a wildly dishevelled creature* with "wind-up mice in the hall"). The 'big nations, small nations' quote is from George Szirtes. 'Hullo!' is full of 'unjust remarks': clearly, for example, some good poets must have won the Pulitzer Prize.

Personism—probably a *good* issue of the *LRB*: Jameson on Raymond Chandler, Eagleton, Marina Warner—usually very good. Pam Brown, Laurie Duggan & I agreed to write something for *Rabbit* magazine, on our shared connection & our three-authored book, *Let's Get Lost.*

Letter to John Forbes—from 2018—intended, initially, to emulate Auden's 'Letter to Lord Byron'—but, Forbes being closer in time, the poem ends up talking to him differently than Auden to Byron.

A Saturday—the Masayo Koike poem: as translated by Leith Morton & published by Vagabond.

Poem (Ascension)—the reader will notice bits of Frank O'Hara early in the poem ("the pony of war", "I am an Indian", etcetera); the line on melancholy is Lord Byron's. Speedboat was *the* great band of Adelaide's 1980s. (The book's title derives from their song 'Oh Well'.) The John referred to in the poem is John Jenkins.

Chapman's Homer—in Darien, Texas, there is no bar called Chapman's Homer. In fact, there is no Darien in Texas.

Reach & Ambition—photos of my overcrowded room, taken by poet friend John Jenkins. 'Loxodrome' is collected in John Tranter's book, *Heartstarter.* He had sent me an early draft.

Shaun Kirby, Deep Farceur—an important, & an interestingly, & excitingly, difficult artist. The poem means to suggest something of his effect: baffling, revelatory, funny & surprising. Used as an acrostic, the title gives the poem a structure.

Richard Grayson—The Life & Times—An account, from 1998, of his then career—written as a farewell—& based entirely on apocryphal stories gleaned by the staff at the Experimental Art Foundation, where I worked, & of which he was the very successful director over an extended period.

As They Come and Korean Mums—Variations For Louise Haselton—the two poems cover some of the same territory and were begun *after* the poem written for Haselton's catalogue—now incorporated—which begins "Now when I / walk around this morning". The title 'Korean Mums' means to acknowledge the women serving in the coffee shop I regularly went to, earlier referred to as Japanese. And Braque—it is funny to think of him as a stoner.

Little Elegy—Cow brand gum is an artists' material, a glue, used a lot in pre-digital era layout & design. Written in 1984 I think.

Star Eyes—the various tunes mentioned (if the reader is *very* curious) are Charlie Parker—'Star Eyes', Art Blakey—'Social Call', Big Jay McNeely—'Boogie In The Front' & 'Tondelayo', Junior Wells—'Little By Little' (from *live at Theresa's*); 'Footprints' & 'Gingerbread Boy' are Miles Davis, then some unspecified Little Walter & Art Blakey; the Magic Sam would have been 'Mole's Blues'. 'This Dark Apartment' is a James Schuyler poem. 'Tondelayo', a choice to be embarrassed at?

Briefing Mary Christie—keeping a peripatetic friend abreast of people & doings in her home town. Her adult children, Millie Dickins (mother of Hector) & Millie's brother Seb Dickins.

"Hi, Small Bug!"—Issa, Japanese poet, 1763—1828. Alex & Penny: friends I'd not seen for many years.

Two Poems for Viv Miller—written to appear in an art exhibition along with works done in collaboration with painter Vivienne Miller. Viv stipulated only that the poems (which are are also acrostics) contain the words "It's very complex." They accompanied (my versions of) an early painting of hers that I very much like: the original is whacky but also coat-trailingly cute &, as the poem has it, 'Freudian'. The Herbert Lom TV series was *The Human Jungle*.

A Travelin' Man—(the title of an old Ricky Nelson song)—written on Bruny Island while reading *Crab & Winkle*, in which Laurie Duggan describes his settling in to the UK. In the poem I wonder, Will he soon return?

Peregian Beach—a beach and suburb near Noosa, Queensland.

Wiesengrund—had been Adorno's surname—until he adopted his mother's maiden name, Adorno. There is play made in the poem—on various ideas of 'the avant-garde', 'kitsch', the 'canon', 'the new'—as held by Aira, Greenberg, Brook, Eliot, Lippard, & Krauss, & Duggan.

www.ingramcontent.com/pod-product-compliance
Lightning Source LLC
Chambersburg PA
CBHW030928090426

42737CB00007B/351